The Land Conservancy of McHenry County

2014 Photo Contest

Art of the Land Amateur Photography Contest Catalog

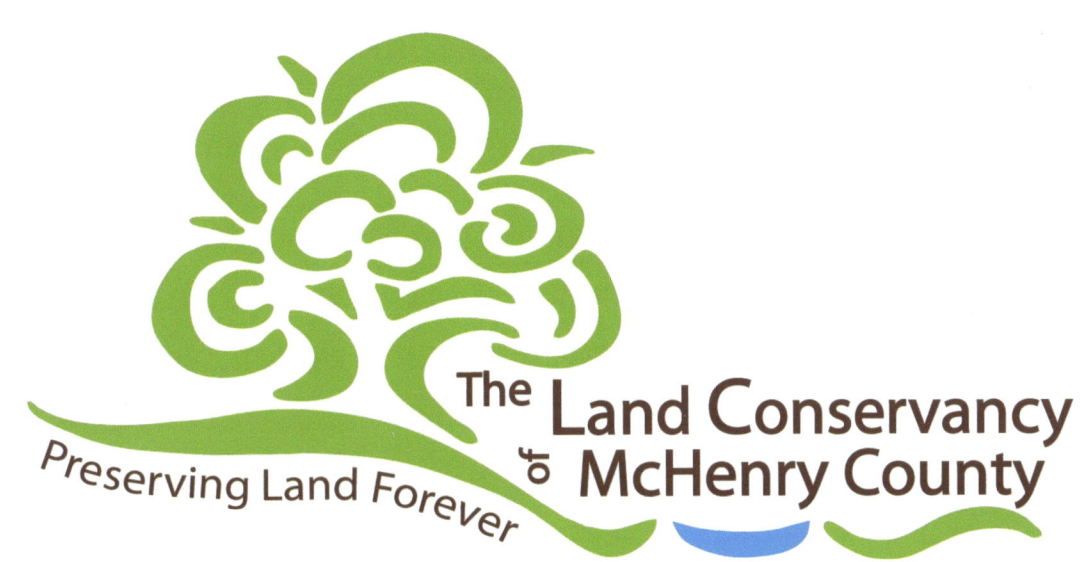

Our Mission:

To preserve natural, agricultural, and scenic land in perpetuity in and around McHenry County by working with individuals, communities and other partners.

About The Land Conservancy of McHenry County:

The Land Conservancy of McHenry County (TLC) has worked with over 100 landowners to preserve nearly 2,100 acres of land across McHenry County. Protected properties range from less than 1 acre to 250 acres in size. Preserved lands include high quality wetland and woodland habitat, farmland, scenic vistas, historic farmsteads, and similar valuable land resources.

The organization accomplishes most of its land preservation work by working with individuals who donate permanent conservation restrictions (also called conservation easements) on their land. Occasionally, individuals donate land to TLC and, on rare occasions, TLC purchases land.

TLC is a local 501(c)(3) nonprofit organization recognized by the IRS and the State of Illinois since 1991. The organization is funded by members, grants, and fundraising events like Art of the Land.

Our Vision:

TLC will be a respected voice for local land and water resources and for the contributions of private landowners to ensure that future generations will benefit from the natural, agricultural, and scenic landscapes that residents enjoy today.

McHenry County will be known for its permanently preserved biologically diverse and irreplaceable natural landscapes, scenic vistas that reveal glacial and agricultural heritage of the area, and its strong community support for conservation. A diverse and growing membership and volunteer base will work effectively alongside staff to nurture and expand the conservation community.

Acorn Lane Conservation Area, Lake in the Hills

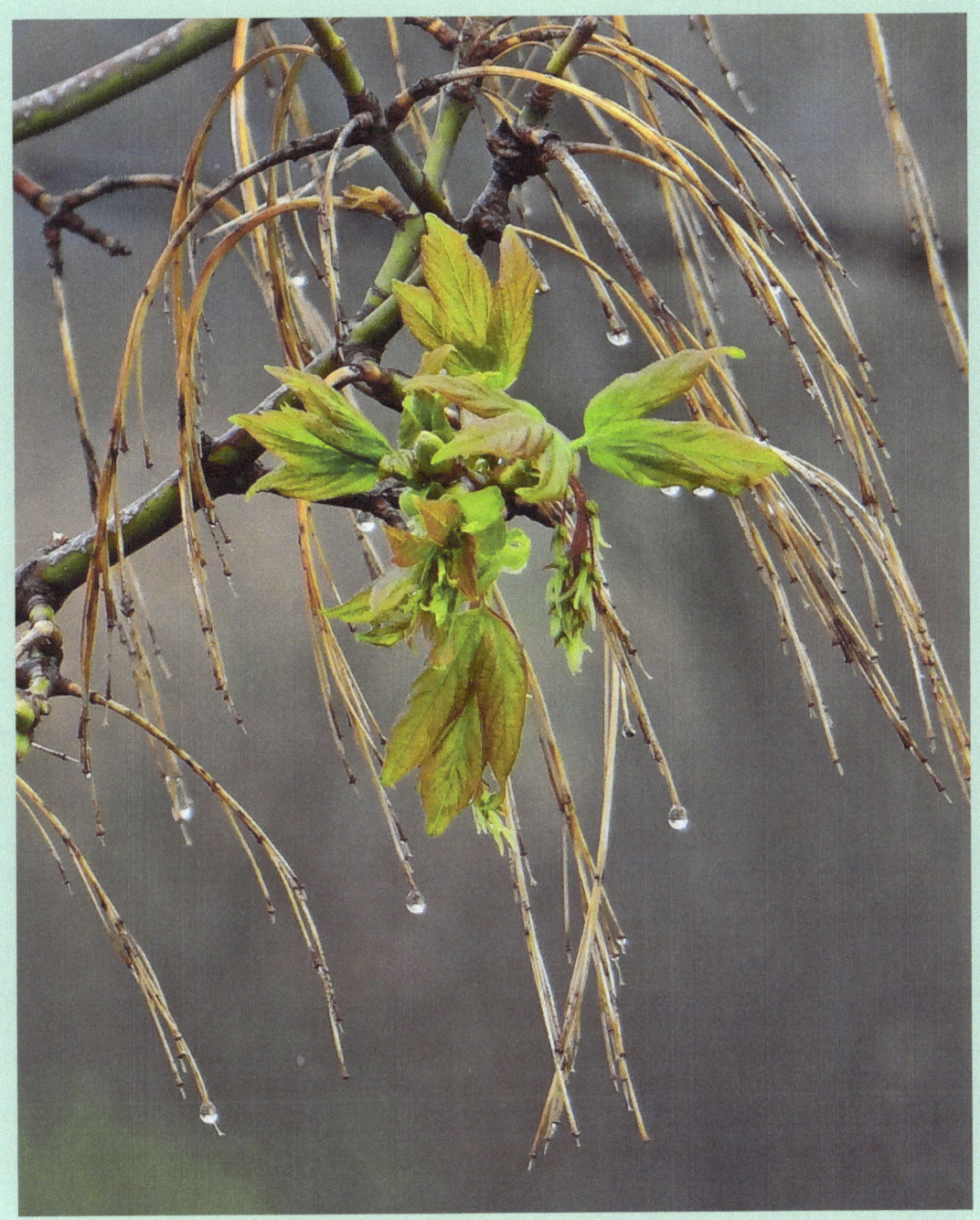

Photographer: Paul McFadden
13 acres donated to TLC in 2006

When you drive down Randall Road, you will see TLC's sign declaring "This Land is Preserved Forever!" This complex of wetlands, prairies, and recent oak plantings will always be here providing habitat and beauty.

Acorn Lane Conservation Area, Lake in the Hills

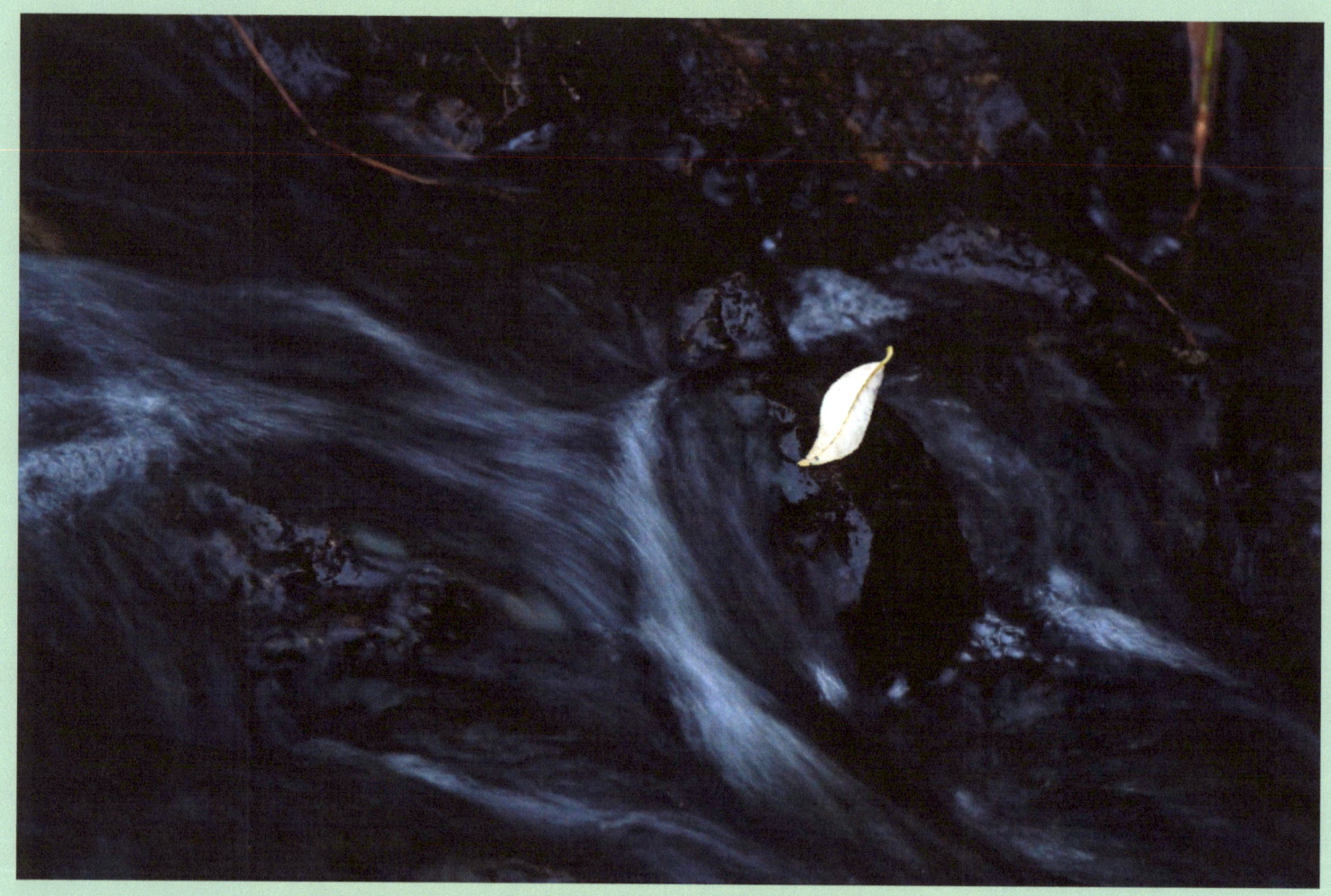

Photographer: Tom Van Der Bosch
13 acres donated to TLC in 2006

This preserve protects a section of Woods Creek and the surrounding wetland, allowing it to stay natural in a heavily developed area.

Anderson Conservation Easement, Nunda Township

Honorable Mention

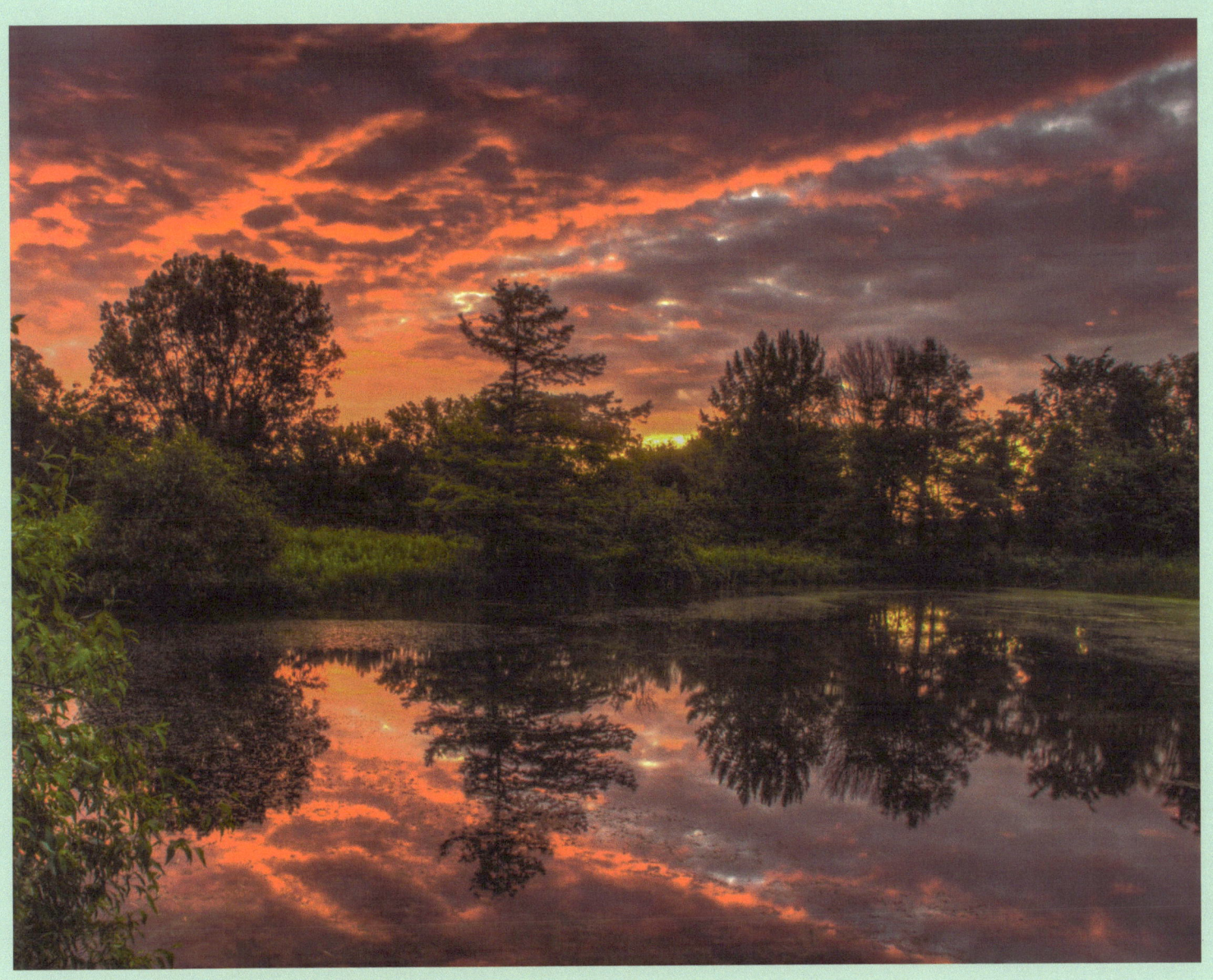

Photographer: Bob Williams
2 acres dedicated in 1994

The Andersons were some of the first people in the county to place a voluntary easement on their land, helping to provide incentive for preservation of the Powers Creek watershed. On the Andersons' easement, paths lead through their backyard ducking around ponds, under trees, and through sweeping patches of native prairie plants.

Apple Creek Conservation Area, Woodstock

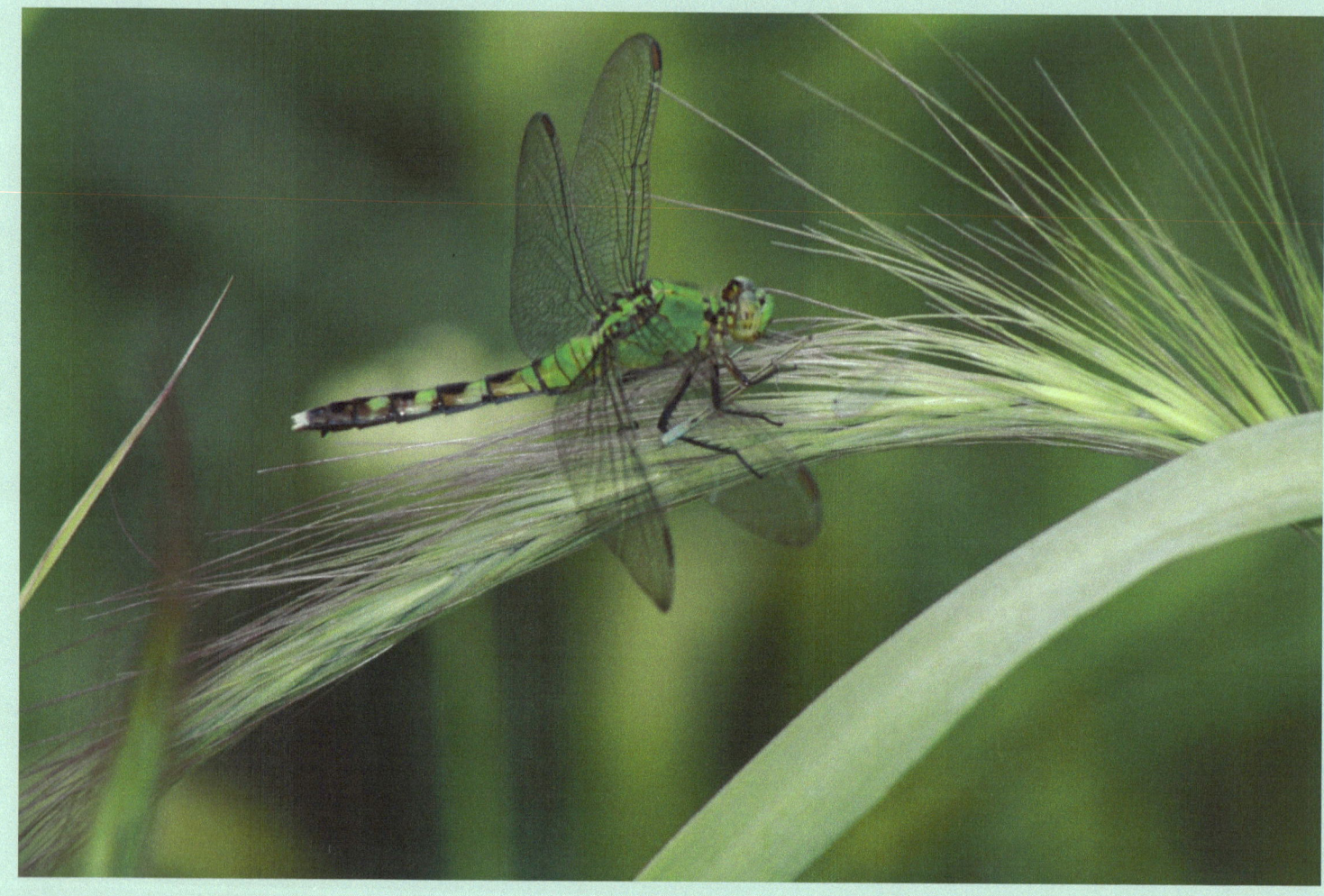

Photographer: Stacy Laskey
36.8 acres dedicated in 2007

Apple Creek is a headwaters stream in the Kishwaukee River system.
As the land is restored, the conservation easement will help to ensure
that this stream will provide high quality habitat for a diversity of
wetland and upland species.

Arvidson Conservation Easement, McHenry Township

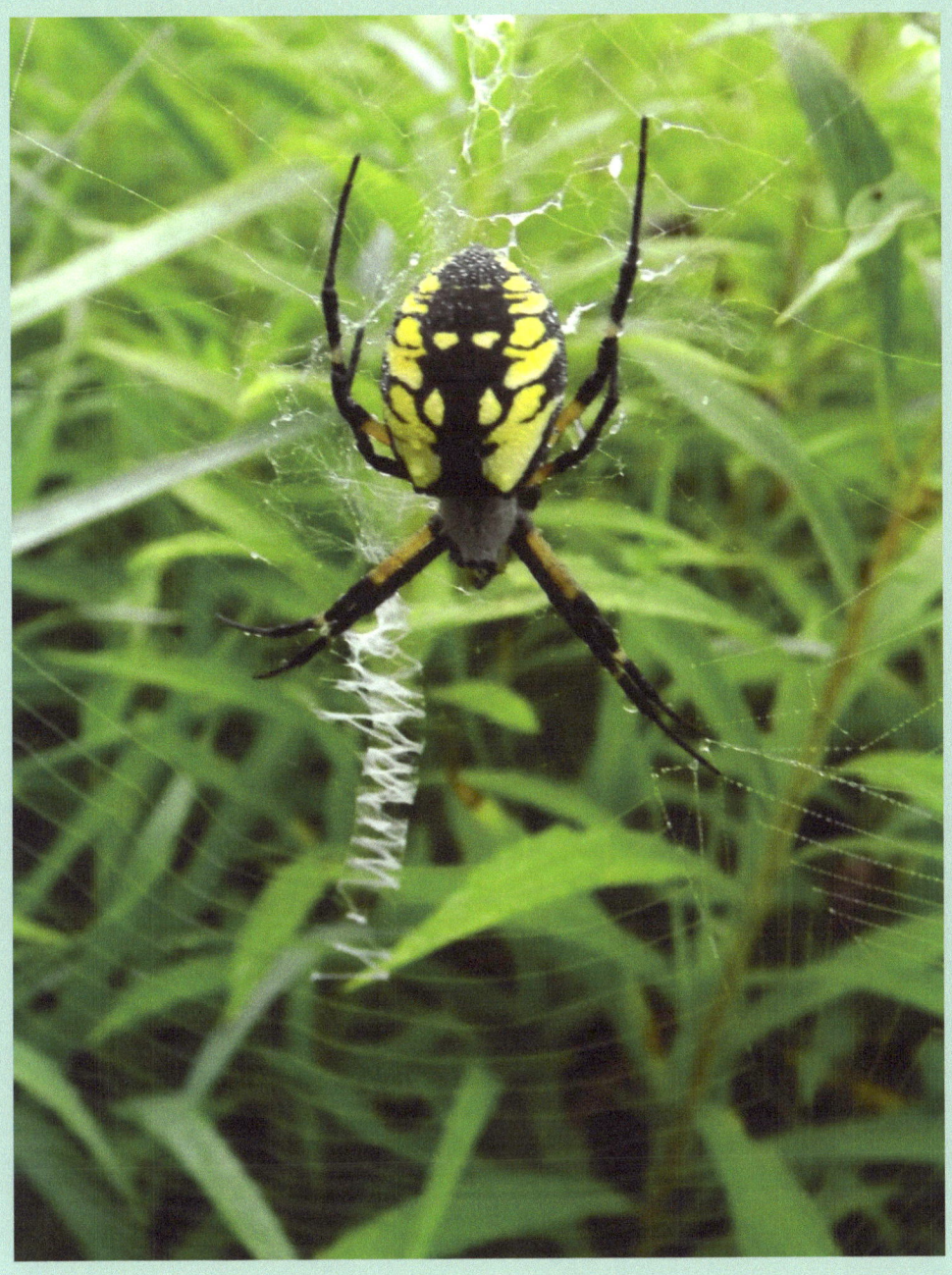

Photographer: Kevin Click
11 acres dedicated in 2009

Don and Dorothy Arvidson own a wonderful piece of land with tall, majestic oaks that likely were here to see settlers arriving in the area nearly 200 years ago.

Barefoot Savanna Conservation Area, Seneca Township

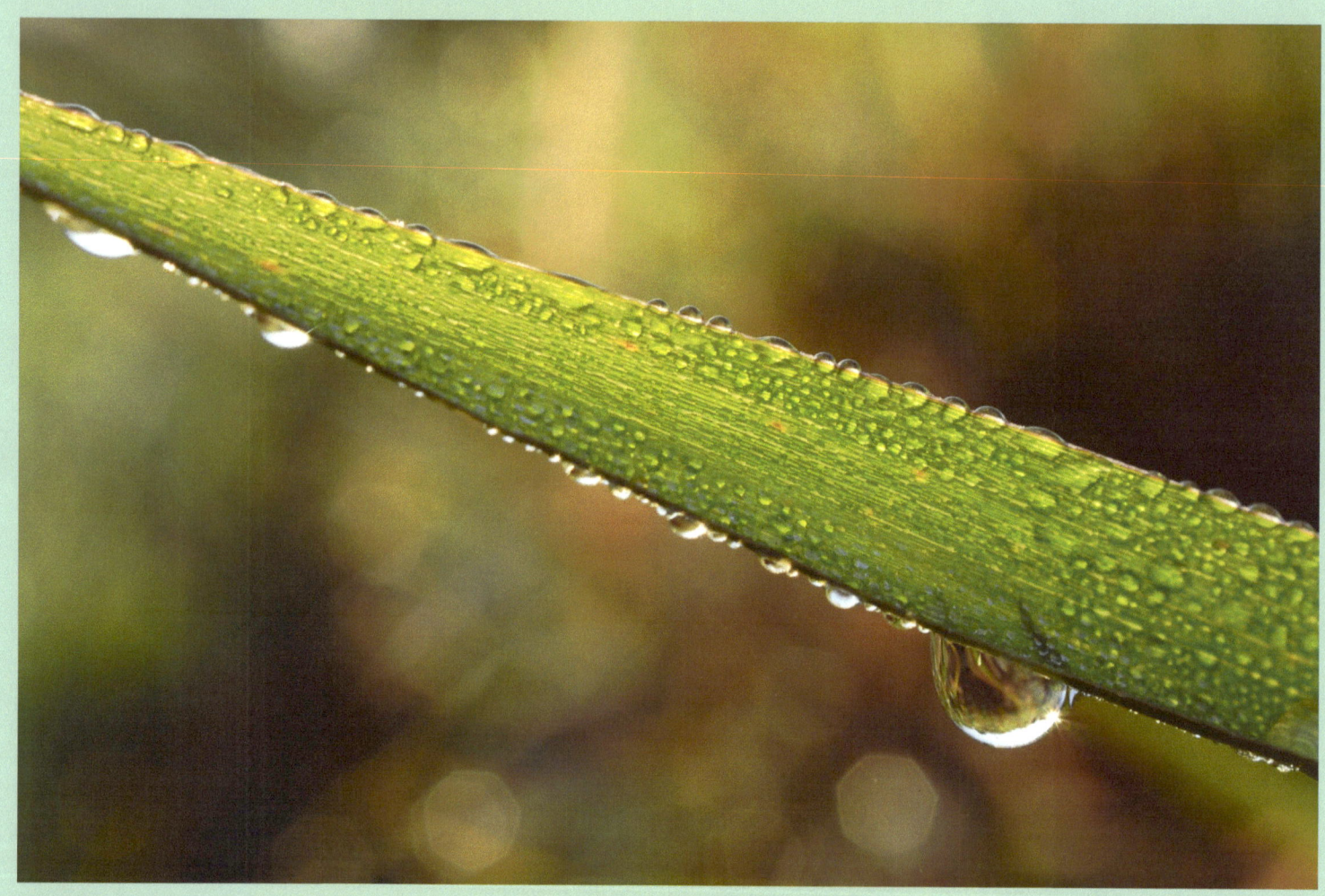

Photographer: Scott Fricke

30 acres donated in 2013

This property was donated by Eric Tauck in 2013. Lots of work has been put into the land to transition it from farmland to a beautiful prairie and savanna where color abounds at all times of the year!

Concannon Conservation Area, Woodstock

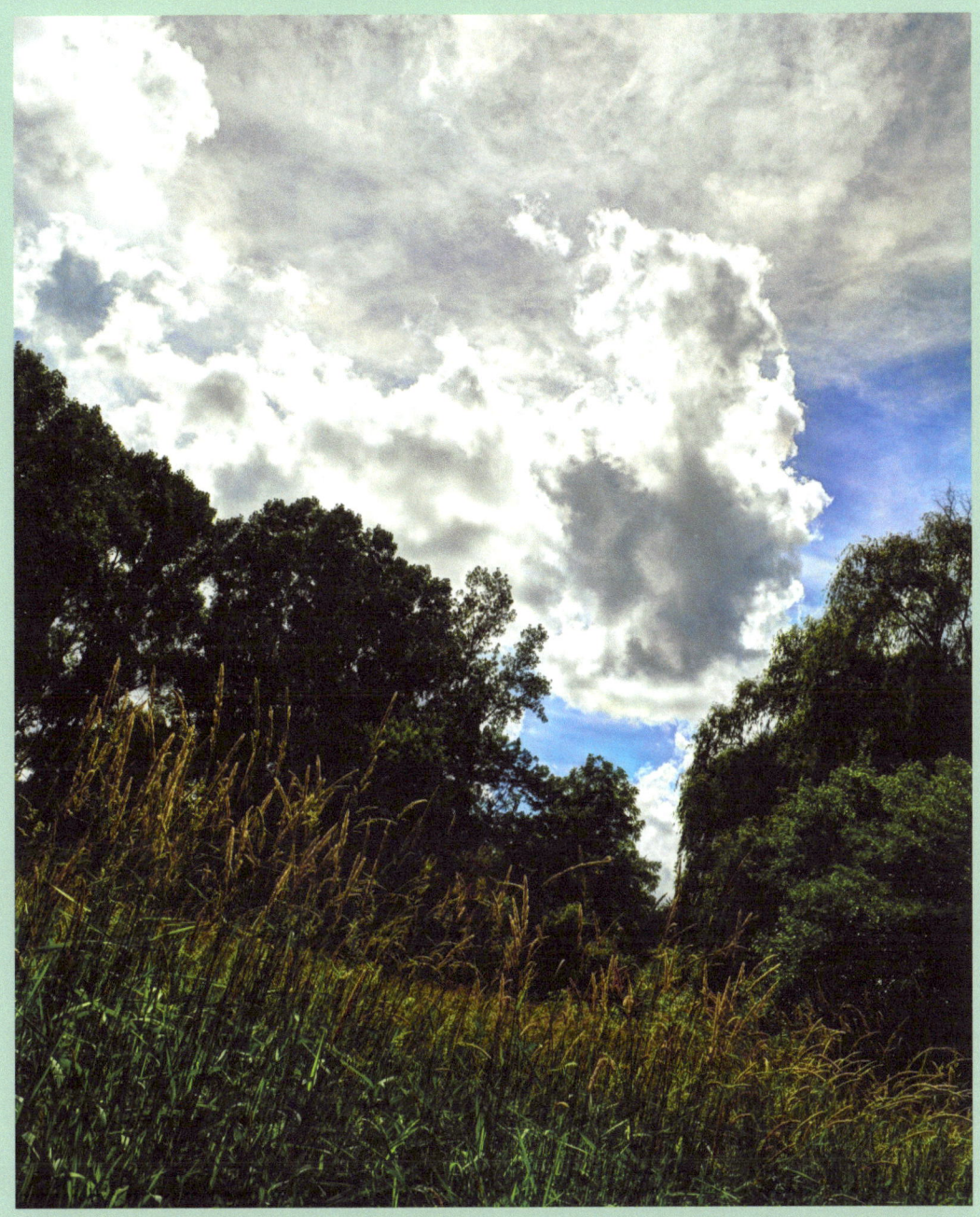

Photographer: Grace Moline
2 acres donated in 2011

On a street corner in Woodstock was a forgotten parcel of land. The owner, Muriel Concannon decided to dedicate it to TLC. Since then, we've been working away at clearing the invasive species, and have been rewarded with finding beautiful native plants that have been waiting for years for someone to care for them!

Country Ridge Conservation Easement, Woodstock
Honorable Mention

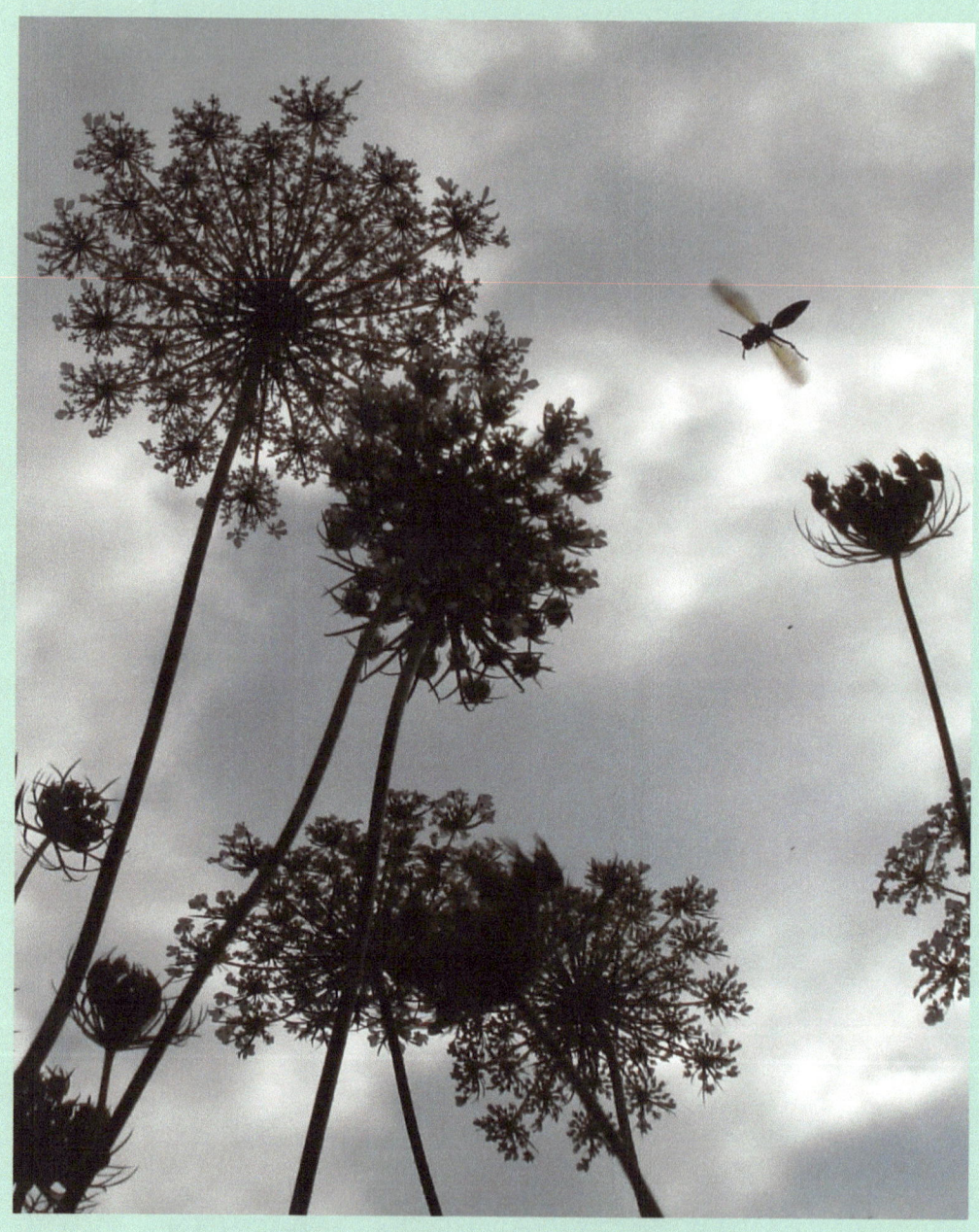

Photographer: Pam Johnson
7 acres dedicated in 2000

Good things really can come in small packages. This easement is a great example of Nature in your Neighborhood with all kinds of plants and animals, all within reach of numerous backyards!

Crowley Sedge Meadow, Alden

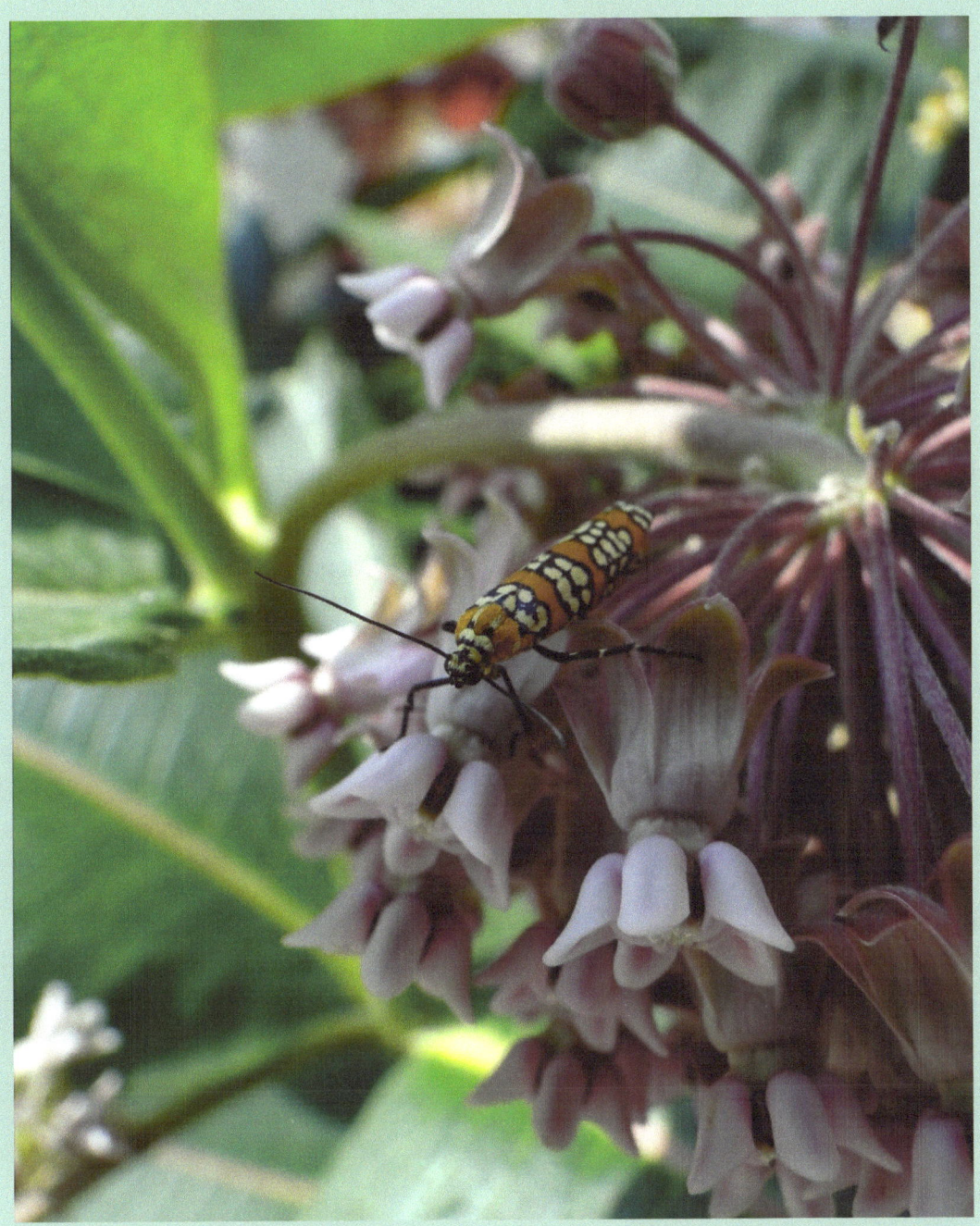

Photographer: Simon Stevens

6.7 acres purchased by TLC in 2004

Crowley Sedge Meadow is the first land that TLC purchased. TLC secured a mortgage to protect this remnant that was too small and isolated for a government agency to buy. Many hours have gone towards brush clearing, weed pulling, prescribed fires, and oak plantings. This little sedge meadow really shines now!

Dutch Creek Conservation Easement, Johnsburg

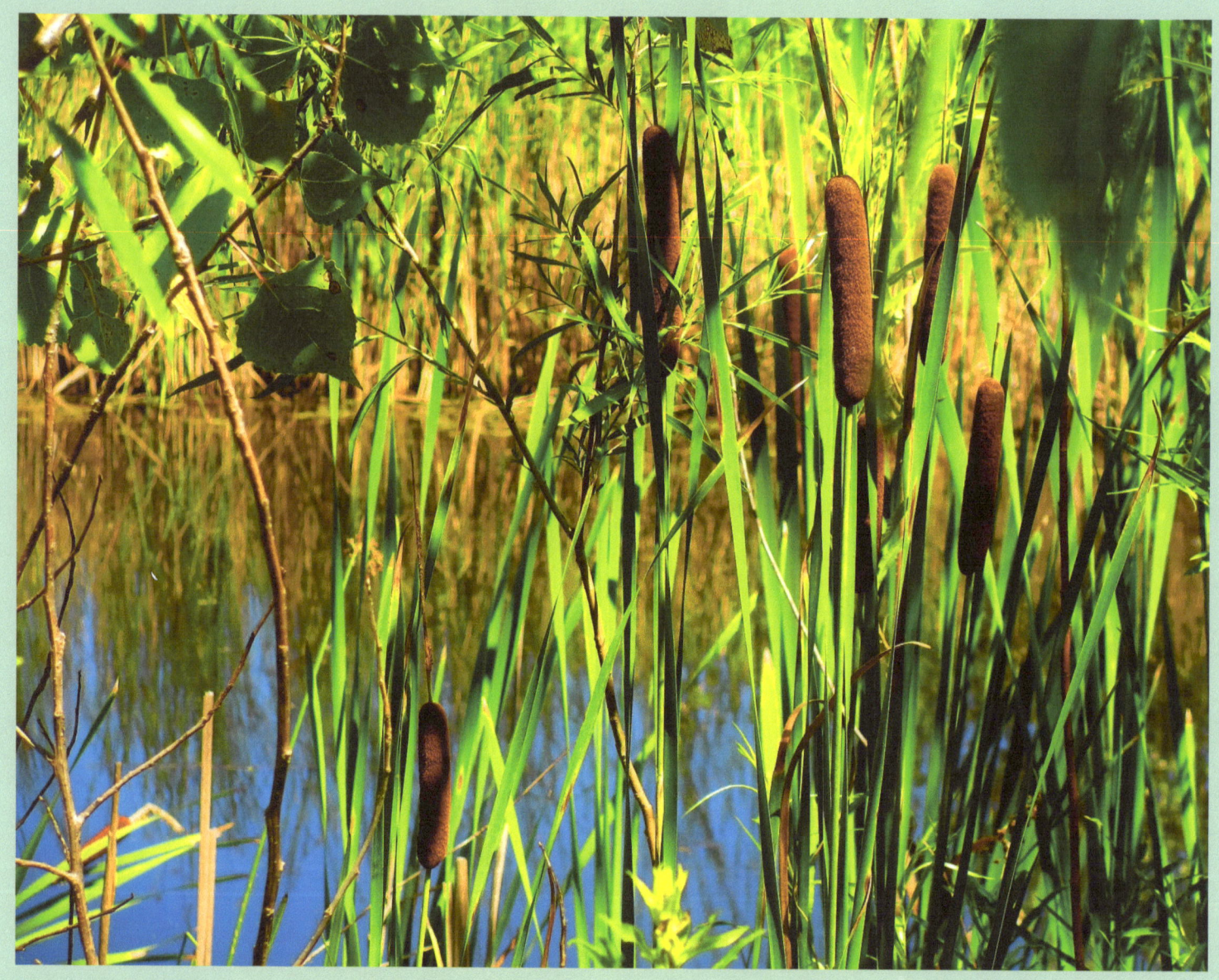

Photographer: Karl Krause

60 acres dedicated in 2007

Located here is one of the highest quality headwater streams in the county- Dutch Creek. The stream flows through sedge meadows, fens, and oak woodlands. Students from the local junior high have planted oaks each Arbor Day for the past six years – over 250 oaks in 6 years!

Dutch Creek Conservation Easement, Johnsburg
First Place Award

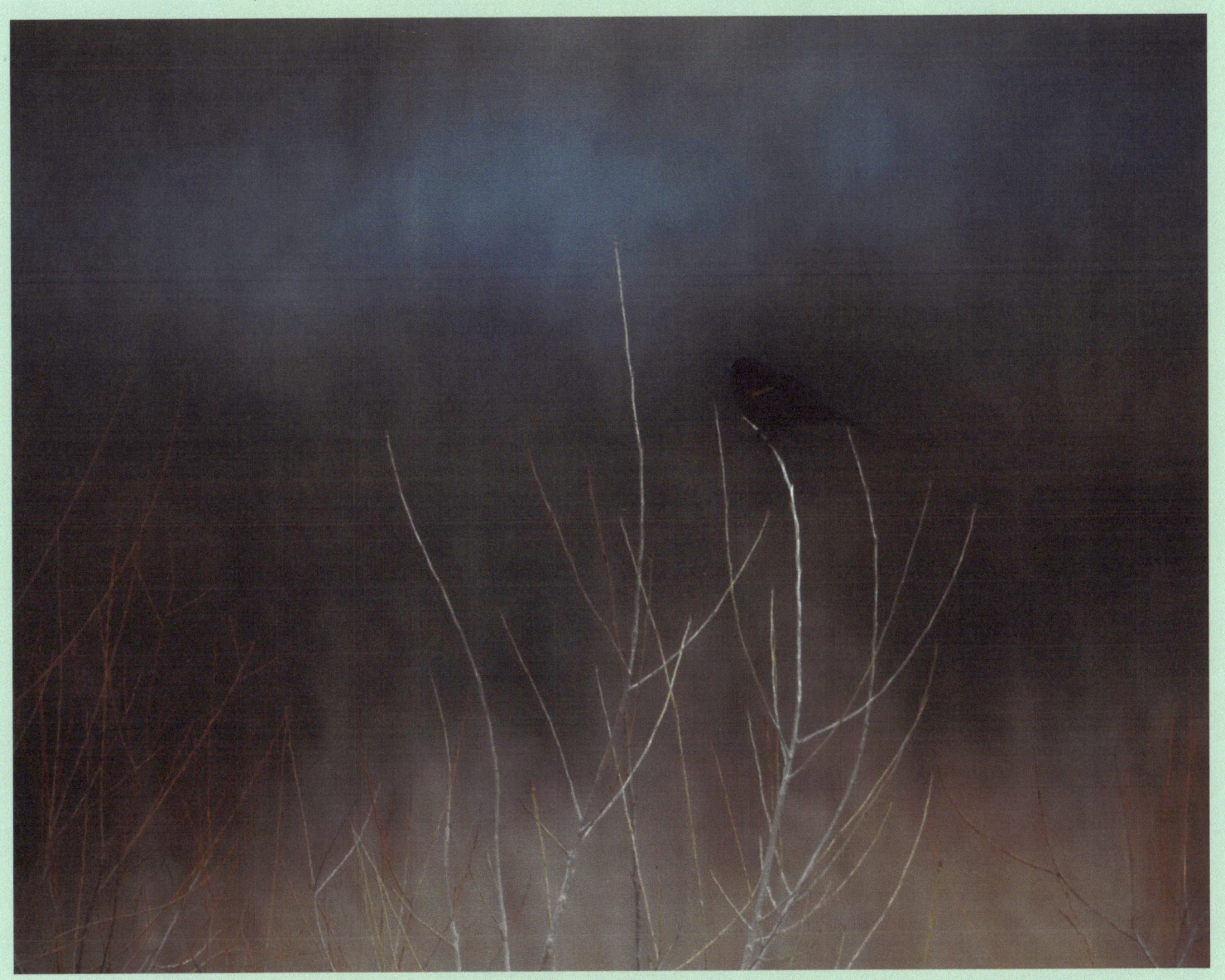

Photographer: Caroline Flaherty

60 acres dedicated in 2007

This easement, located within the Dutch Creek Estates subdivision, is part of a larger complex of land protected by TLC, the McHenry County Conservation District, and the Village of Johnsburg. By working together with other organizations, we can protect the 170 native plant species that call this their home.

Dutch Creek Conservation Easement, Johnsburg

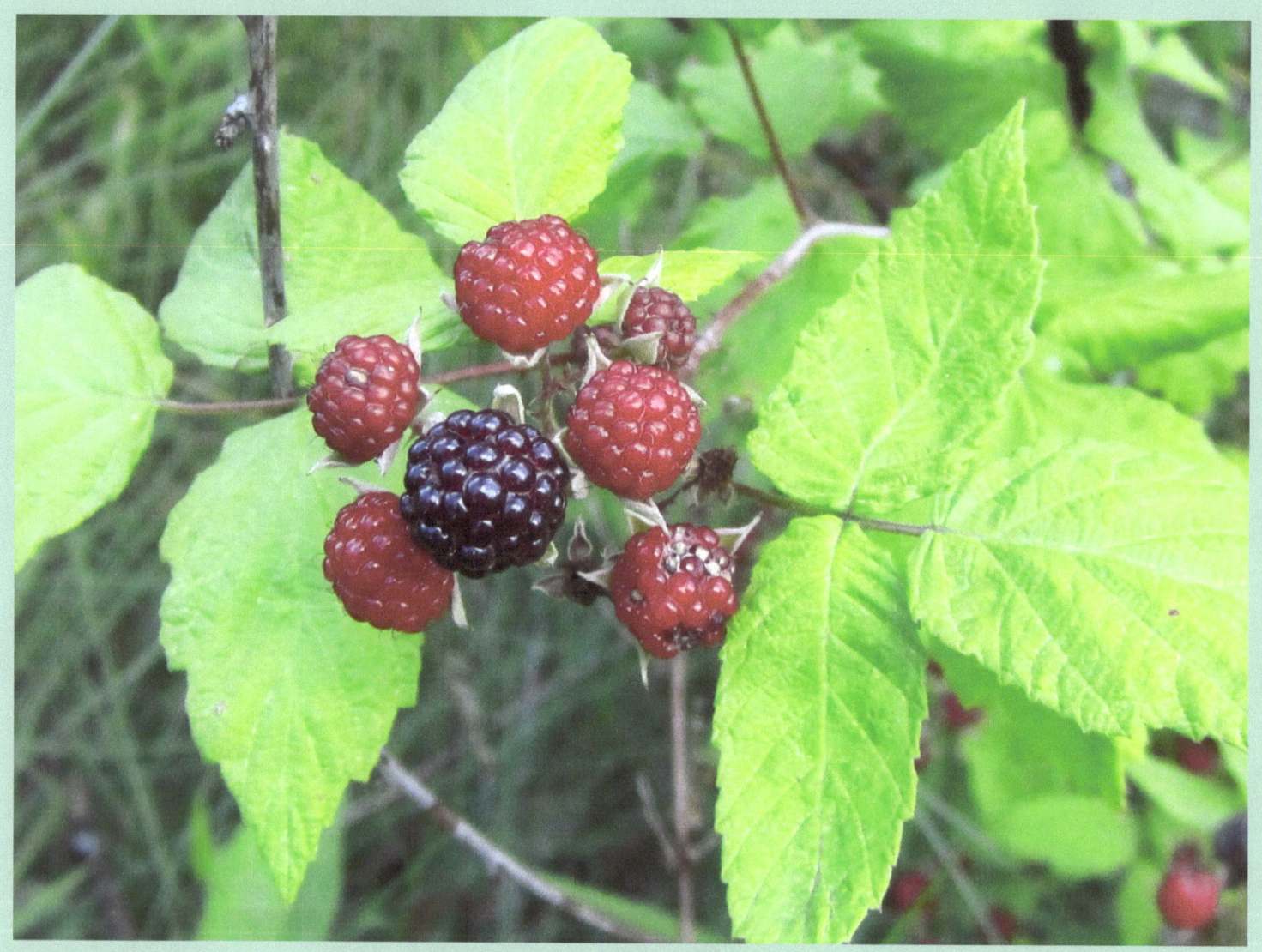

Photographer: Mary Jo Stedman
60 acres dedicated in 2007

Site steward Bob Roe restores this land, because of "My general love of being outdoors and tackling physical challenges, my desire to contribute to creating as healthy an environment as possible for humankind and all living creatures, and my hope to nurture a spirit of caring for the land in my community that will inspire future generations to continue this journey."

Finch Farm Agricultural Easement, Greenwood Township

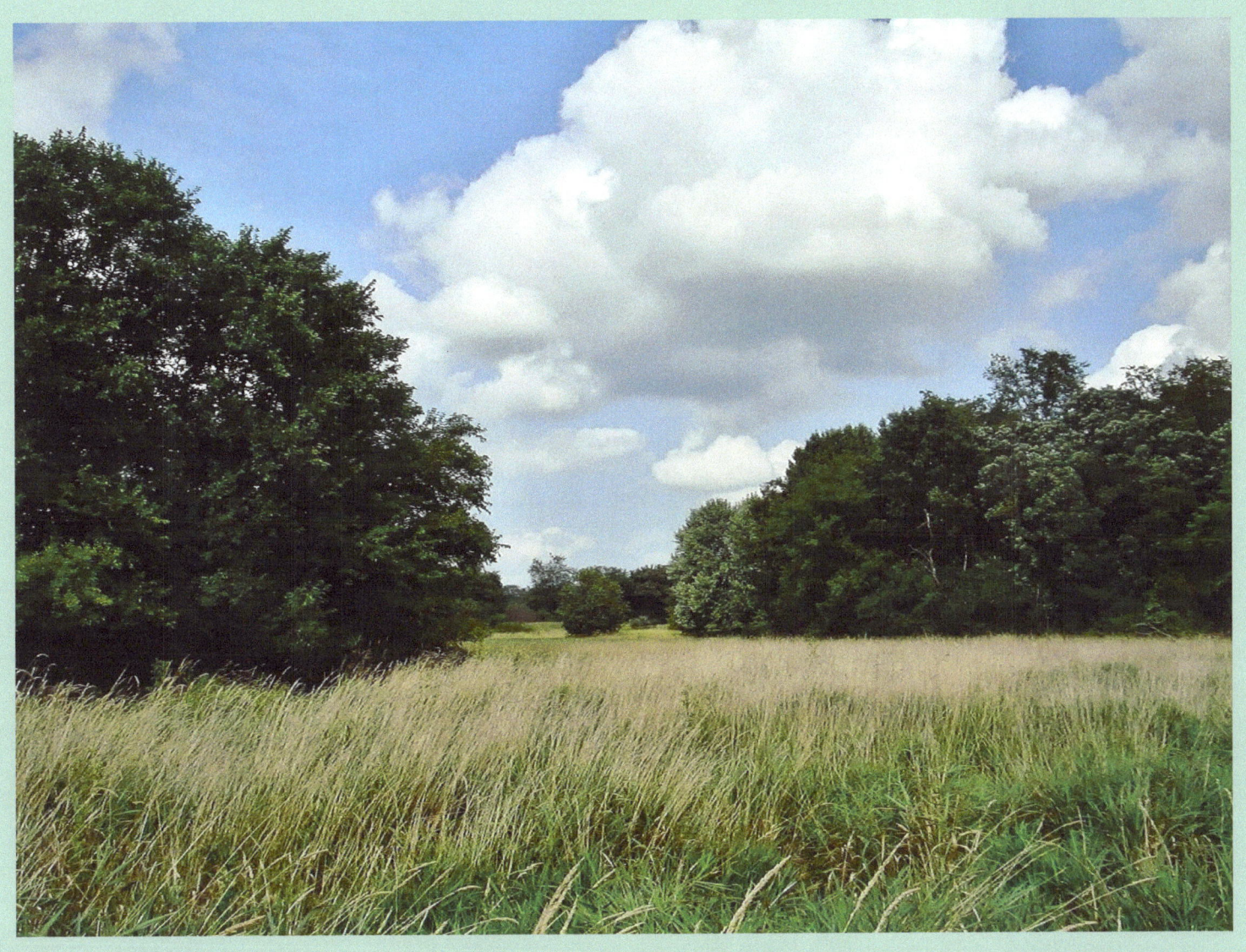

Photographer Jerry Rygg

149 acres dedicated in 2007

When John Finch originally acquired this land for farming in 1862, these trees were already standing there tall and proud. Thanks to the foresight of his great-granddaughter, Josephine Elsen, the trees and the farmland can keep on growing as they have for more than 150 years.

Harvard Gateway Nature Park

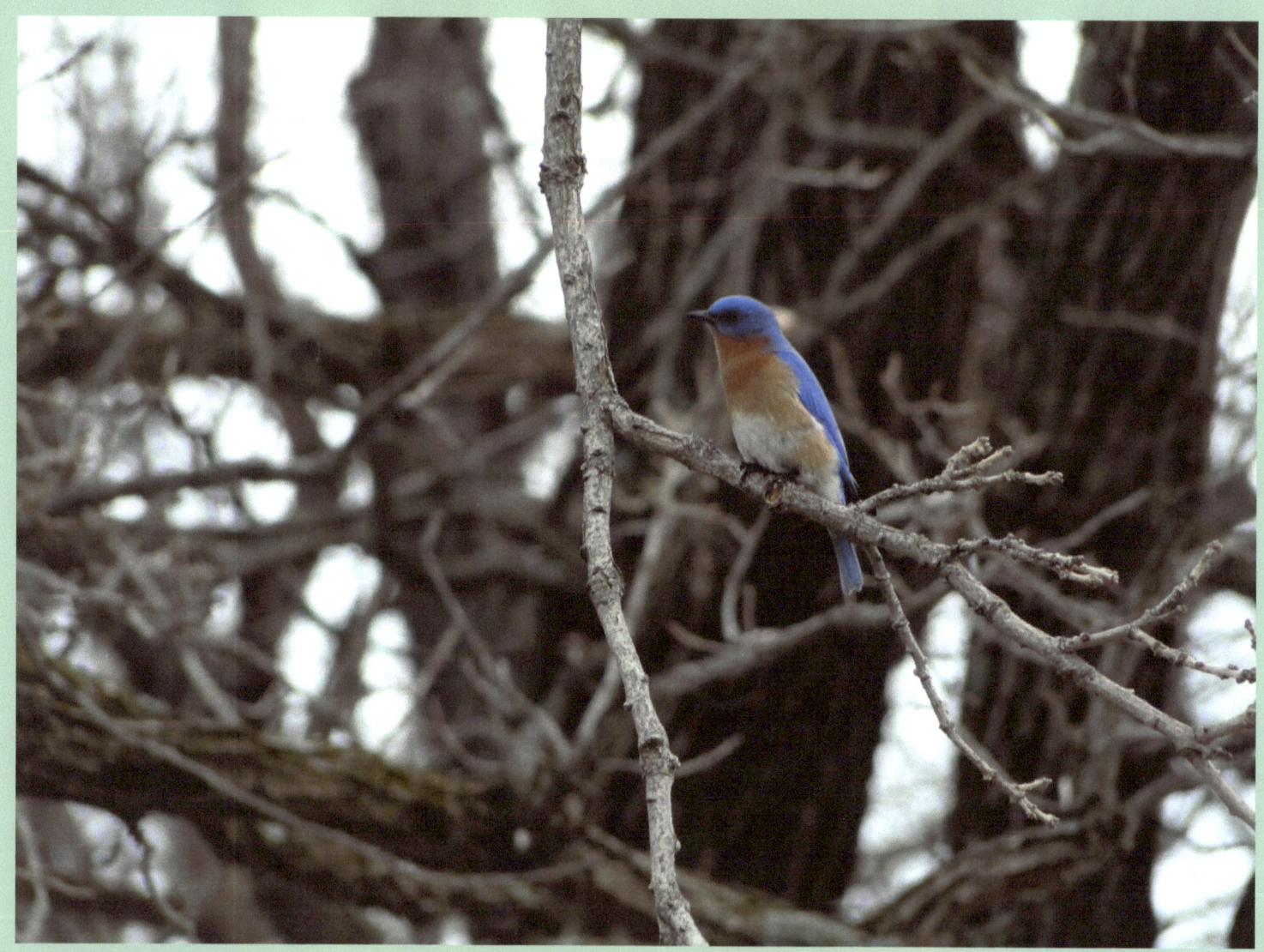

Photographer: Corie Stevens

17.5 acres purchased in 2012

Little treasures keep popping up at this site as restoration continues.
Each year the prairies, savannas, and wetlands offer new and
exciting views and a great diversity of color. The open woodland now
invites uncommon species like bluebirds!

Harvard Gateway Nature Park

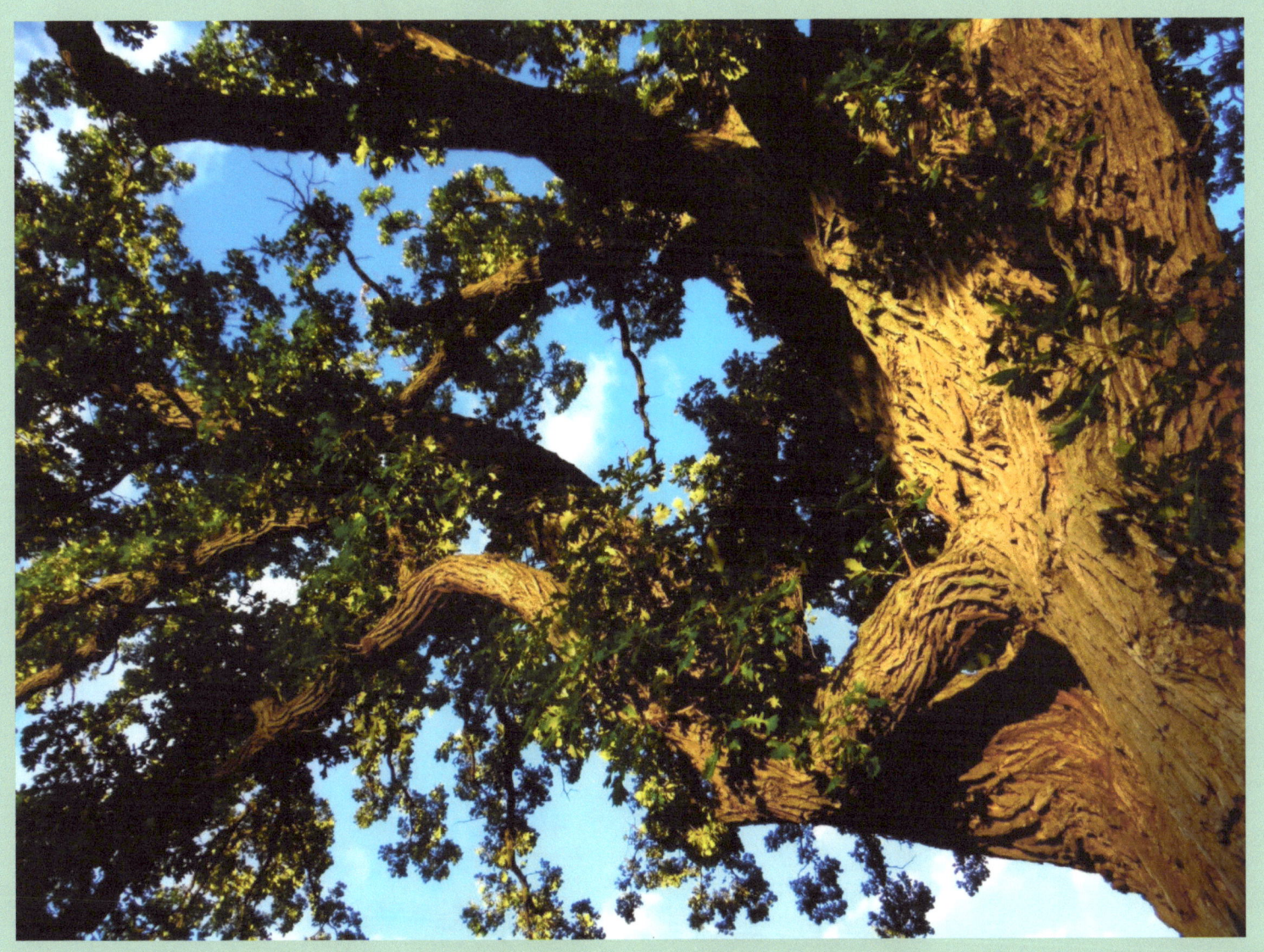

Photographer: Amy Peterson

17.5 acres purchased in 2012

When TLC acquired this site we discovered a true gem: the county's largest white oak, estimated to be 400 years old. Now that most of the invasive brush has been removed, the oak limbs can spread out and reach for the abundant sunlight.

Hennen Conservation Area, Woodstock

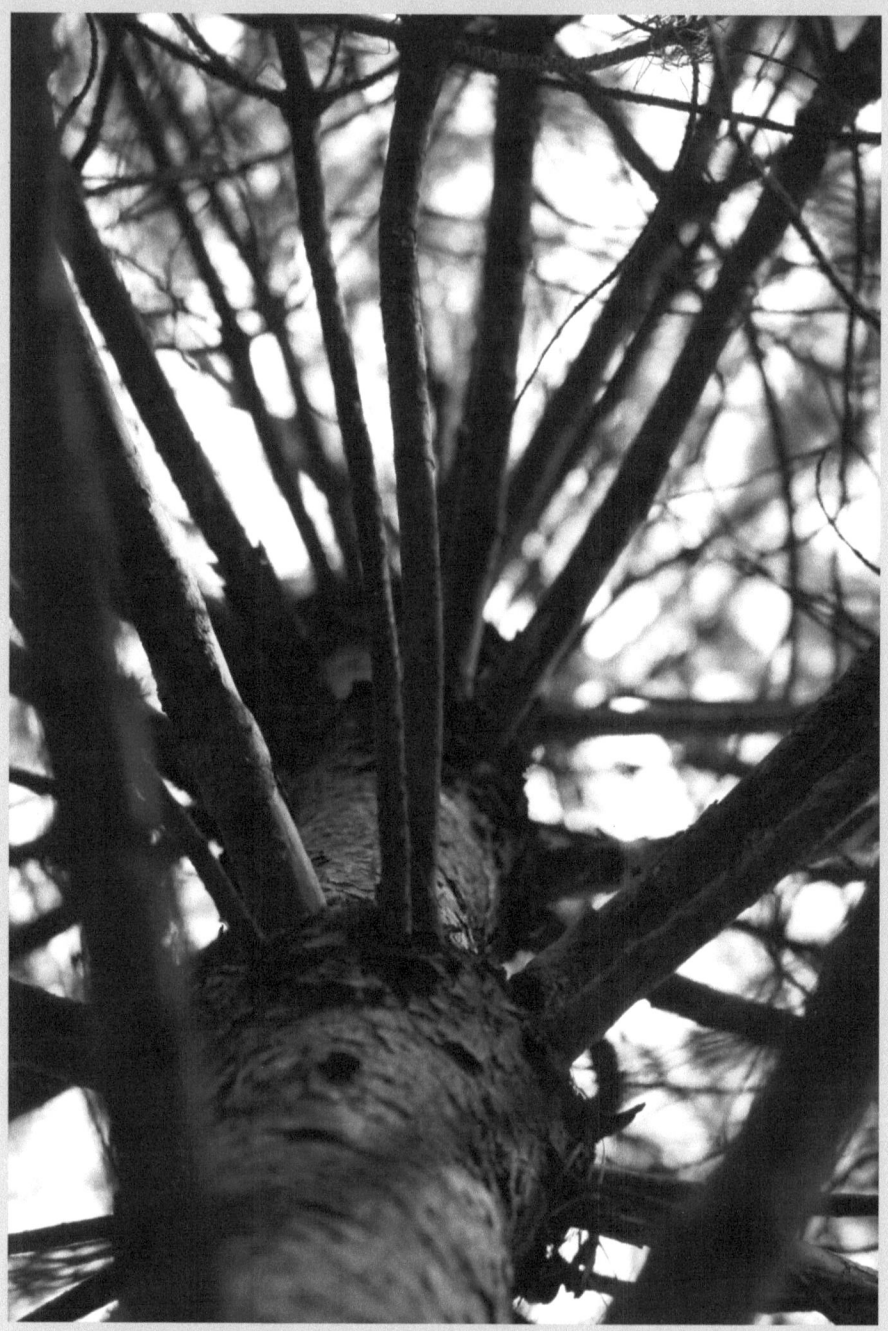

Photographer: Susan Creath

25 acres dedicated in 2008

Phyllis and Tony Hennen acquired this land in the early 70s, planting thousands of native hardwood seedlings. They donated the land to the City of Woodstock as a public park, and TLC moved their offices into the farmhouse.

Hennen Conservation Area, Woodstock

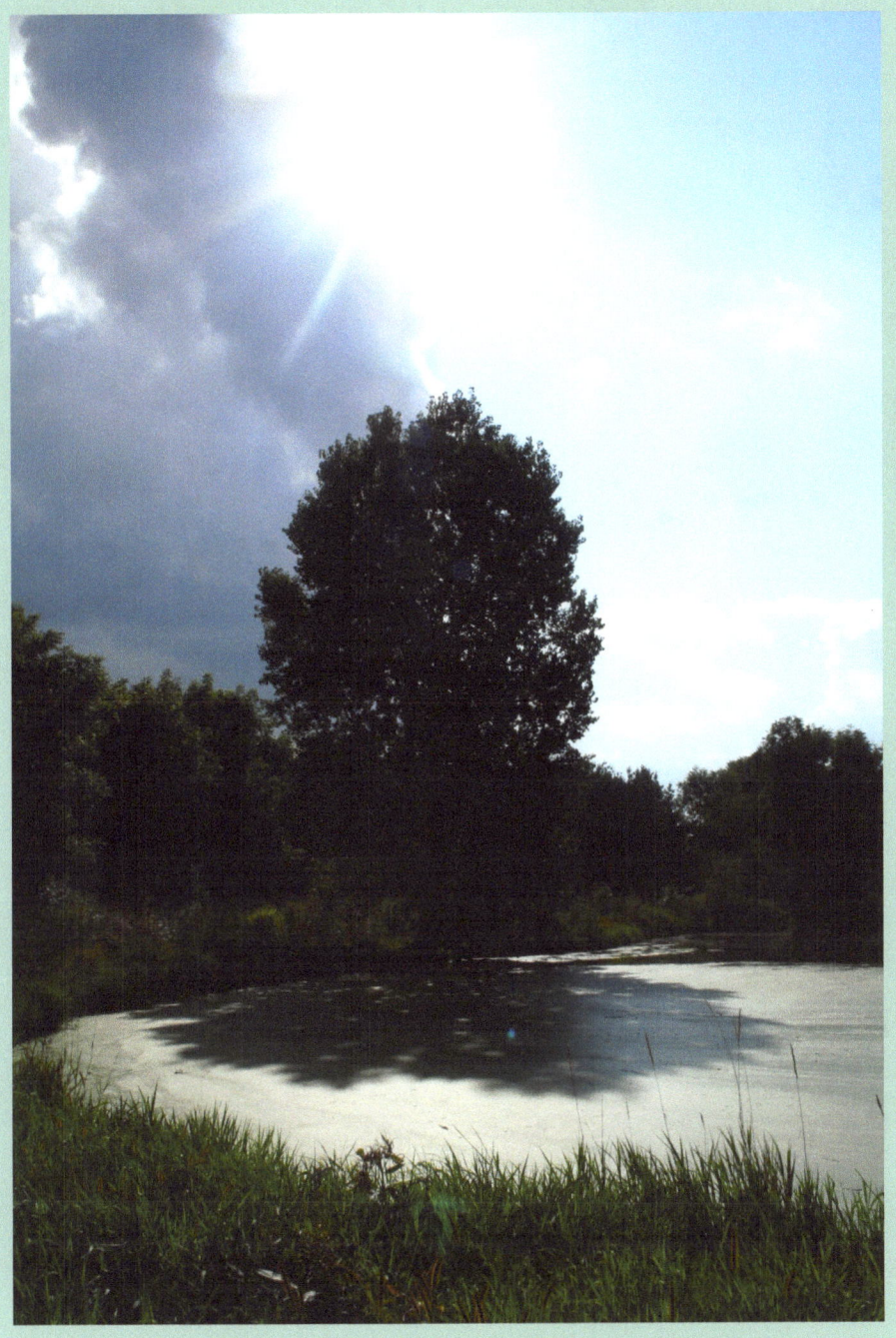

Photographer: Weston Creath

25 acres dedicated in 2008

The ponds found throughout McHenry County are not only pleasing to look at, they help provide food and homes for our local birds, amphibians, and insects. Green herons, king fishers and sandhill cranes are found at Hennen Conservation Area.

Hidden Marsh Conservation Easement, Hebron
People's Choice Award, Saturday

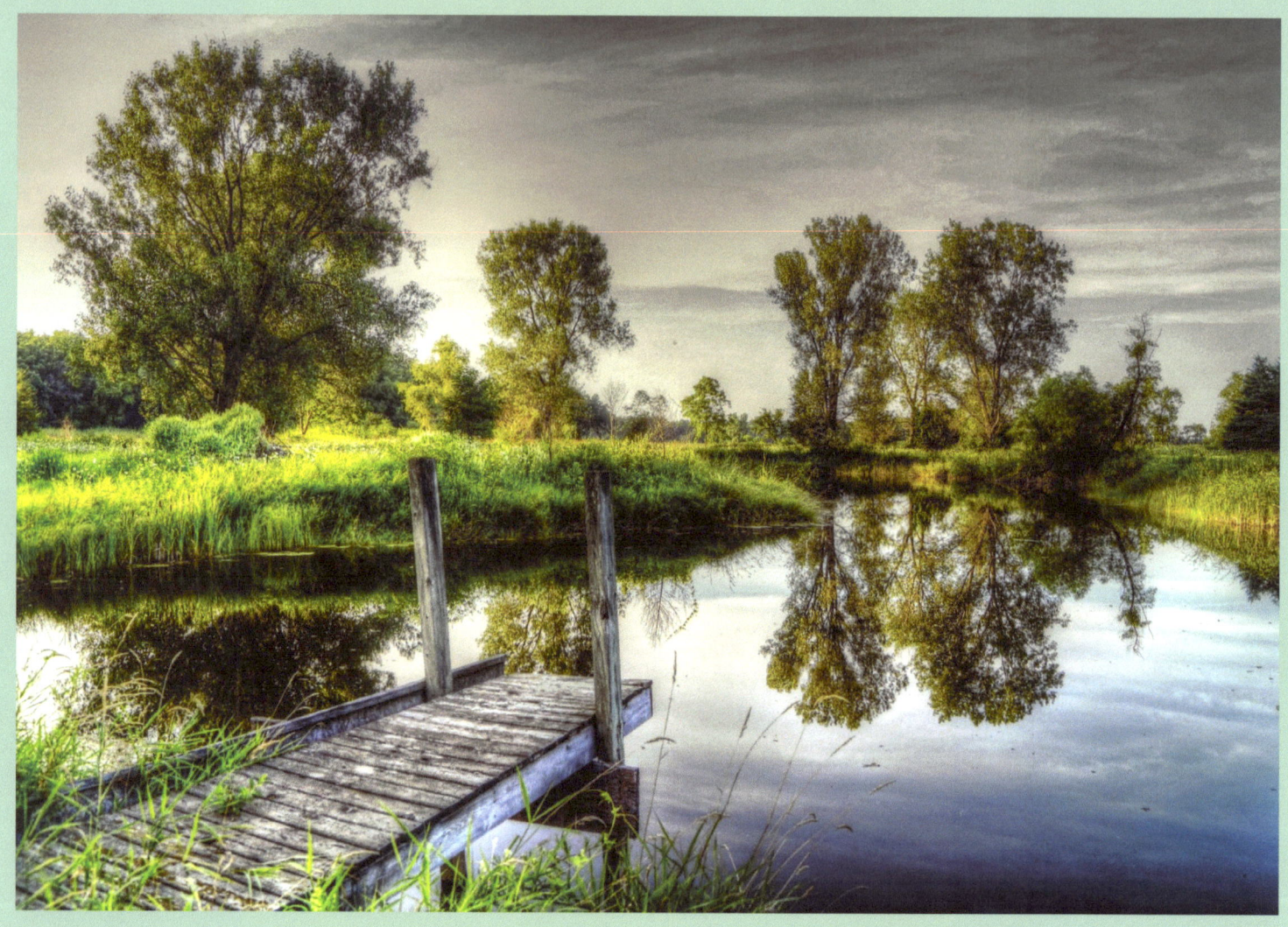

Photographer: Rob Peterson

25 acres dedicated in 2007

Two glacial kames and an esker will never be mined for gravel. A sedge meadow will never be filled for development. An oak woodland will never be cleared for a farm field. That is the power of this conservation easement.

Hunter Conservation Easement, Ringwood

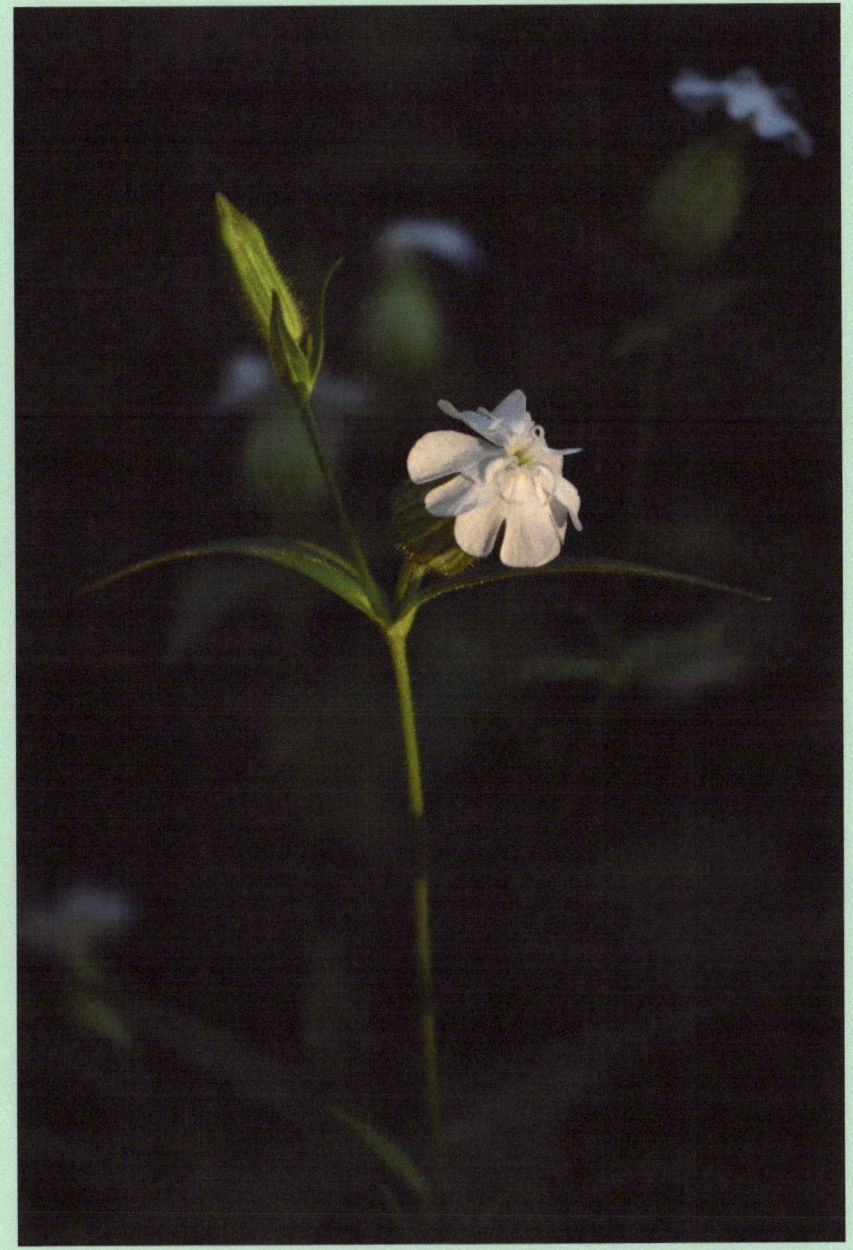

Photographer: Patricia Morgret

14 acres dedicated in 2009

The Hunters ensured this majestic oak woodland will be available for future generations to enjoy, both though a conservation easement and brush clearing restoration efforts. Located next to McHenry County Conservation District's Glacial Park and the Arvidson Conservation Easement, a large area of this ancient forest is now protected forever.

Kaskel Conservation Easement, Hebron

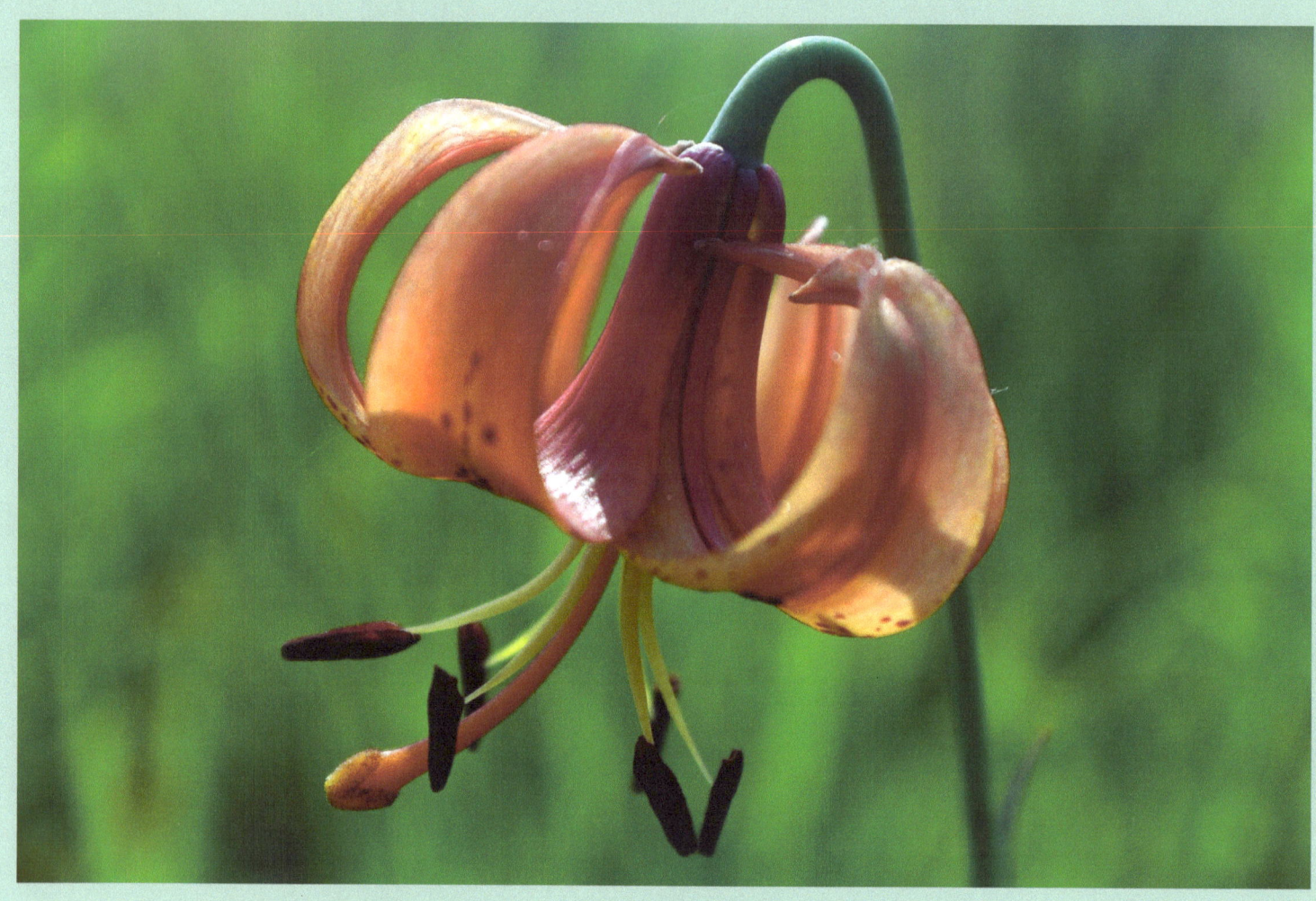

Photographer: Bryan Krause

15 acres dedicated in 2004

The Kaskel property is one of the highest quality sedge meadow and wet prairie habitats remaining in the county. Owners Jack and Maurine Kaskel of Red Buffalo Nursery have done an amazing job keeping this area maintained!

Pistakee Preserve, McHenry Township

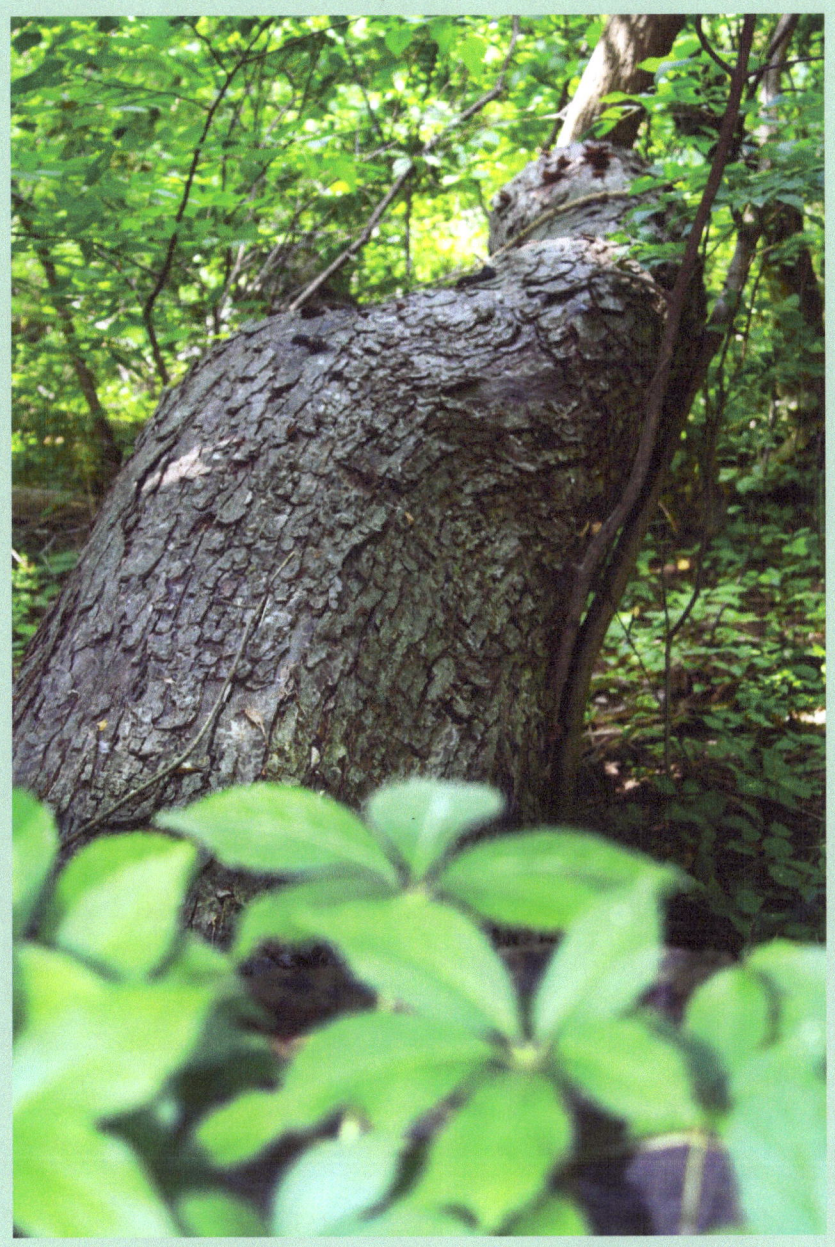

Photographer: Brian Durkin

3 acres donated in 2009

This land along Pistakee Lake has been in the same family since the 1800s. The three Olson sisters agreed on a donation to TLC, protecting the natural lakeshore and a lagoon in an area where mowed lawns line most of the lake.

Prairie Ridge Fen Conservation Easement, Woodstock

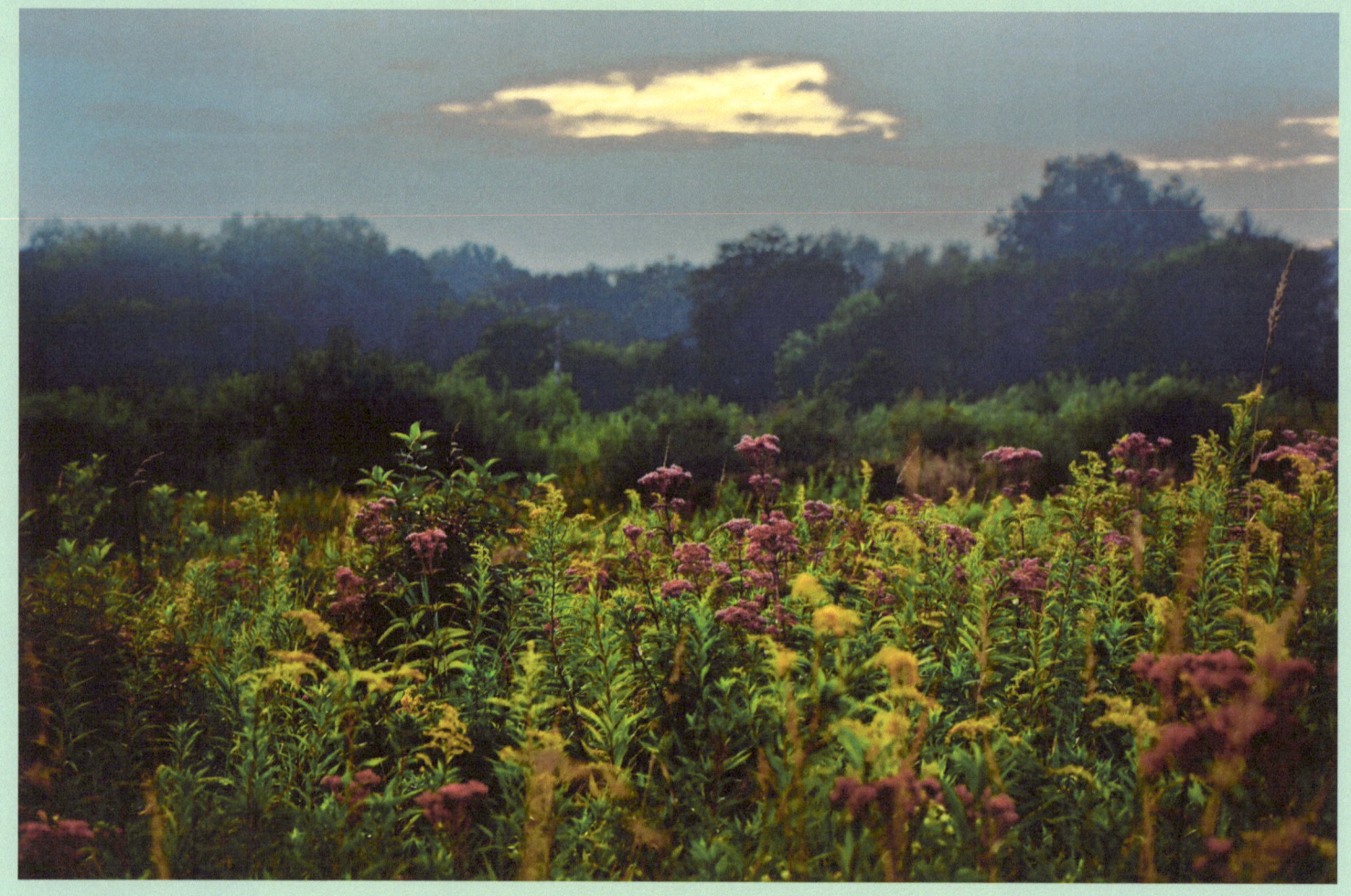

Photographer: Todd Weber

9 acres dedicated in 1996

Prairie Ridge Fen was a tangle of buckthorn and reed canary grass in 1996 when TLC was granted a conservation easement and long-term management agreement by the owner, the City of Woodstock. Today it is a living testament to the power of restoration, harboring uncommon species like turtlehead and the Baltimore Checkerspot butterfly!

Remington Grove Conservation Easement, Johnsburg

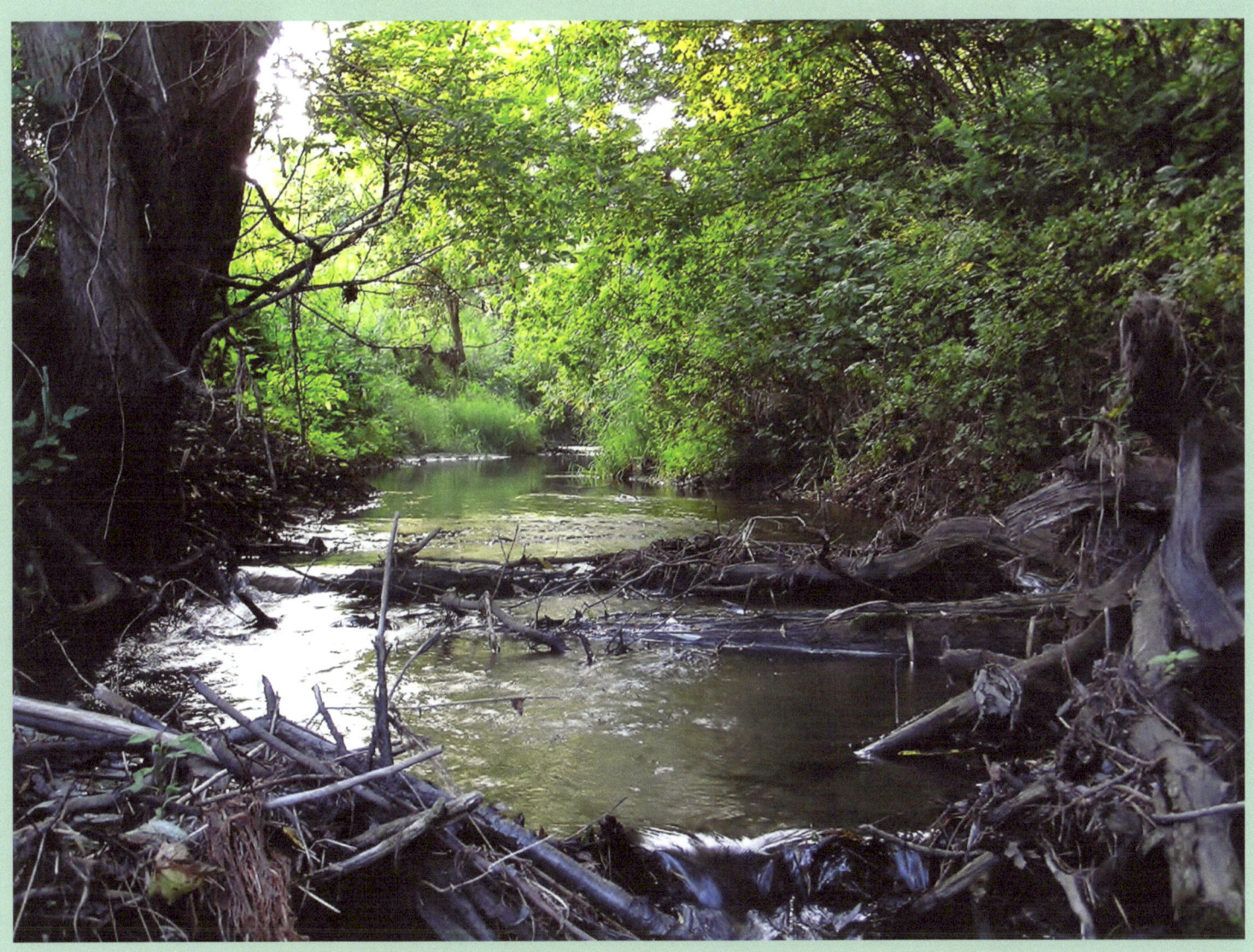

Photographer: Tracy Bordis

23 acres dedicated in 2012

Recently TLC was able to preserve another branch of Dutch Creek, creating even more long lasting protection for this watershed.

Remington Grove Conservation Easement, Johnsburg

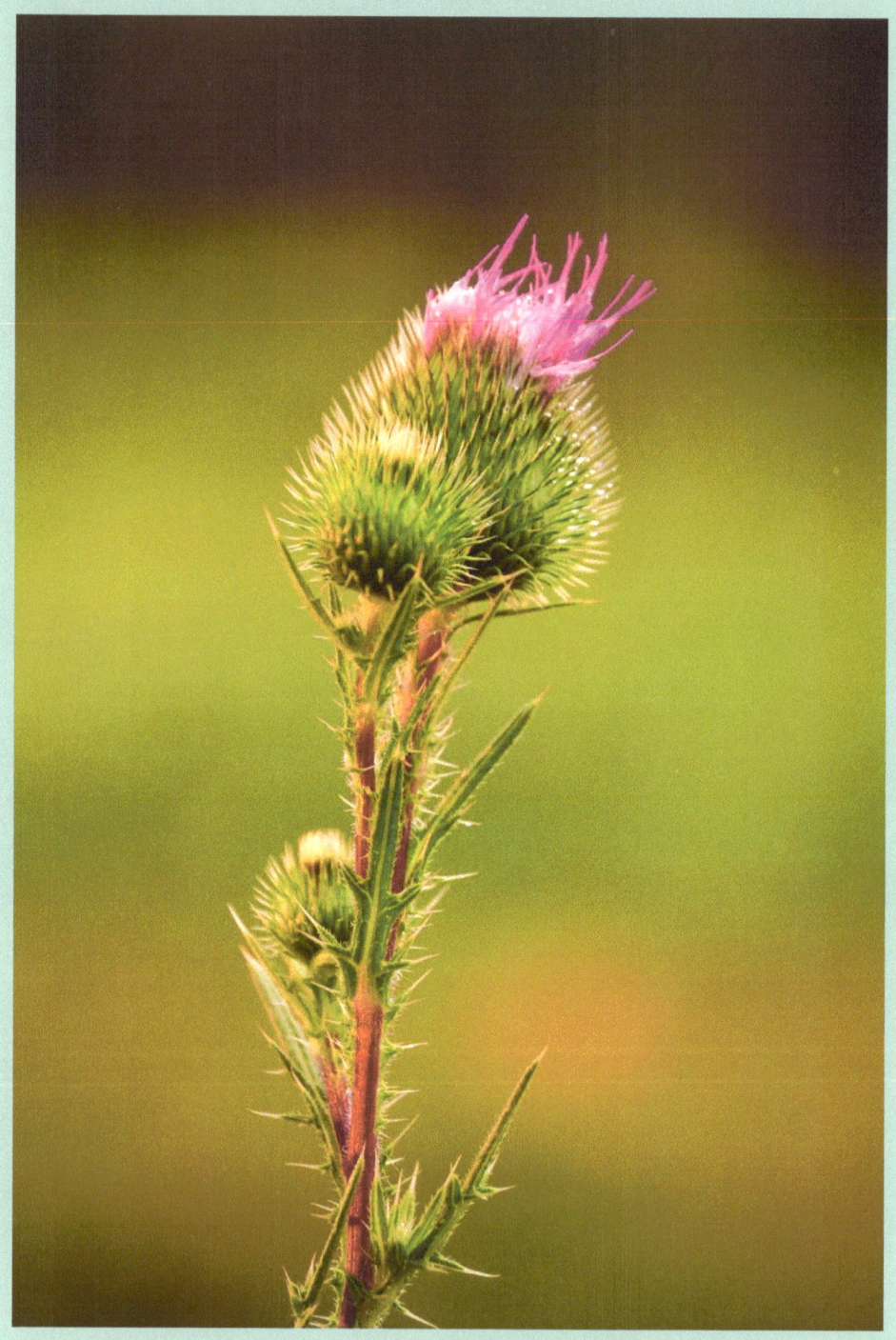

Photographer: Albert Castellanos

23 acres dedicated in 2012

Although this easement is still in the early stages of prairie development, it harbors a great diversity of life and habitat.

Ryders Woods, Woodstock

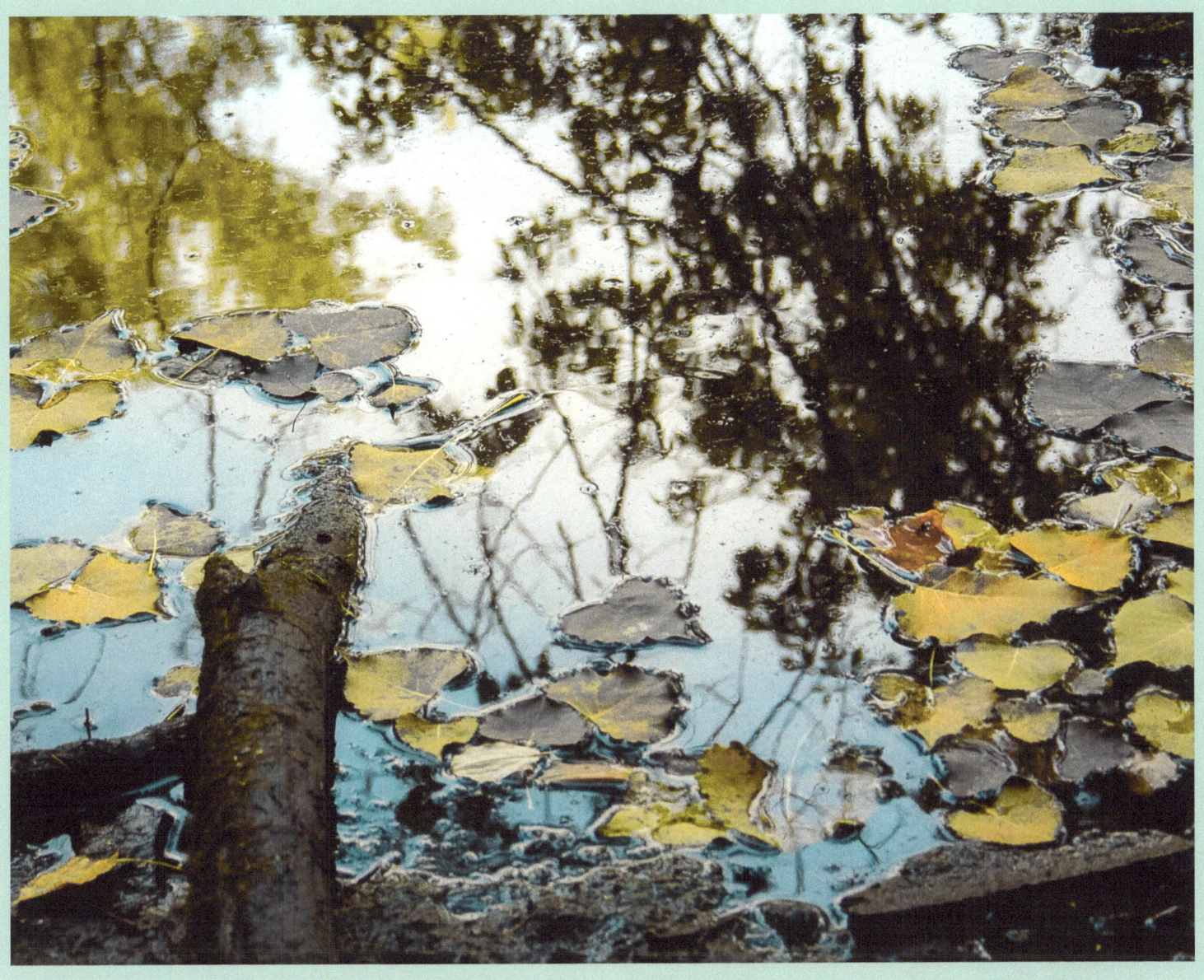

Photographer: Michelle Myshkowec

22 acres owned by the City of Woodstock,
managed by TLC since 2006

A group called "Friends of Ryders Woods" was active in the 1970s working
to ensure this gem located blocks from the Woodstock Square would
provide peaceful enjoyment to residents forever. Today, the City of
Woodstock, TLC, and local volunteers work together to maintain the woods.

Ryders Woods, Woodstock

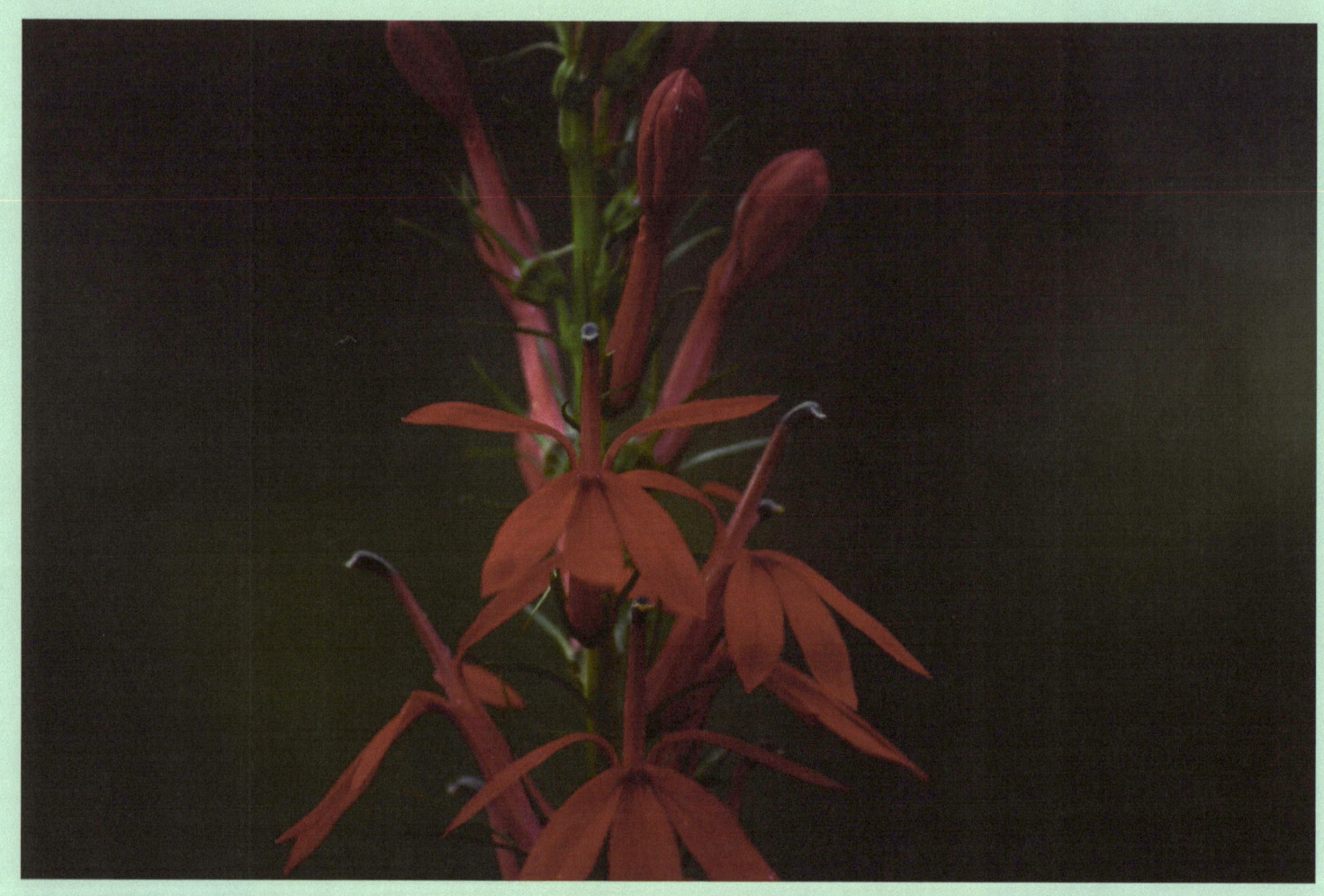

Photographer: Zach Grycan

22 acres owned by the City of Woodstock,

managed by TLC since 2006

By managing the buckthorn and other invasive species, TLC and volunteers have transformed the woods into an open and inviting sanctuary for people and wildlife.

Simon Conservation Easement, Alden

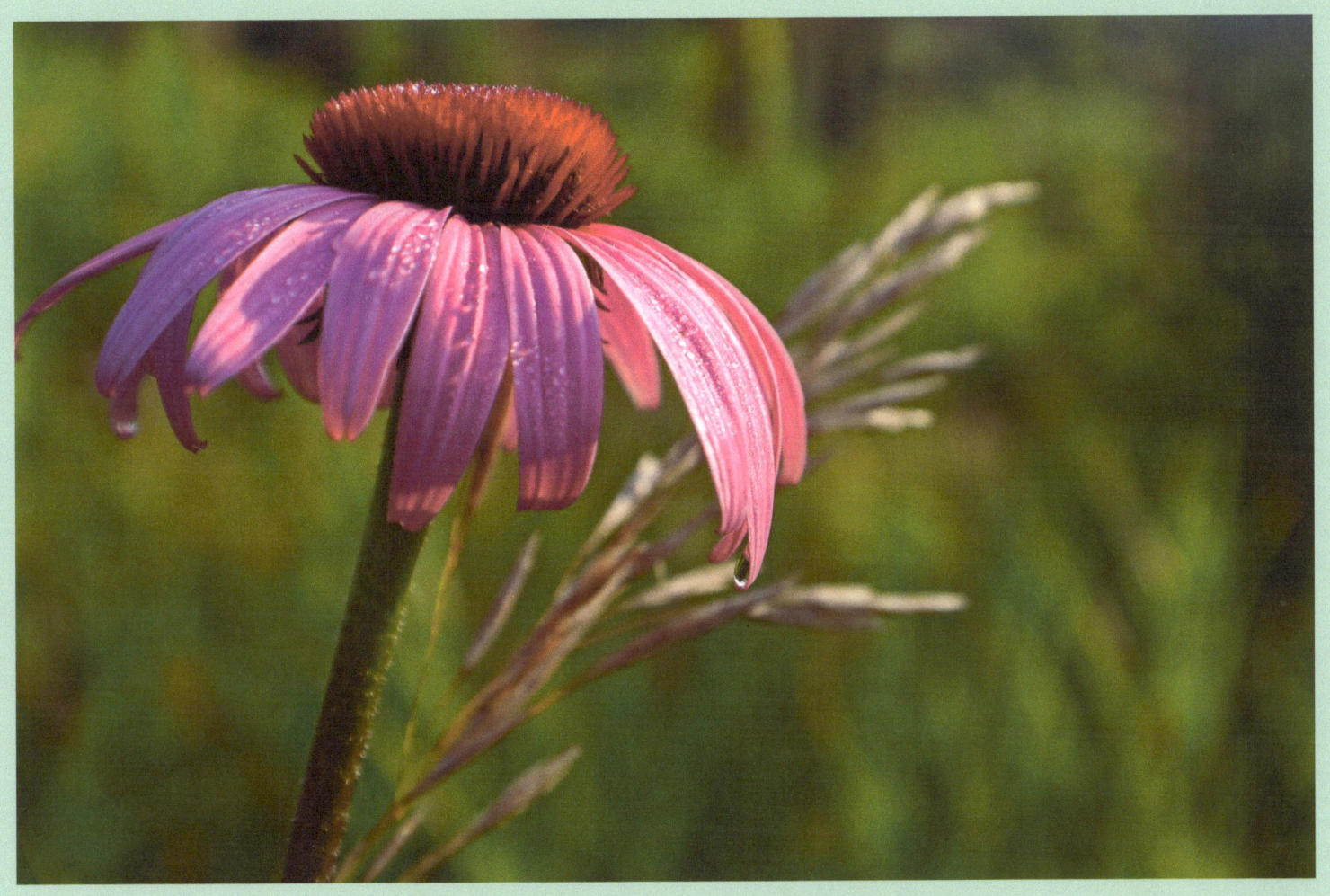

Photographer: Pat Krause
1 acre dedicated to TLC in 2007

Stephanie Shetler-Simon and Jerry Simon acquired a beautiful stretch of land with the Nippersink Creek running through it. The rolling topography offers a spectacular view of the creek and all the wildflowers blooming along it--thanks to many hours of hard work!

Sobczak Conservation Easement, Greenwood

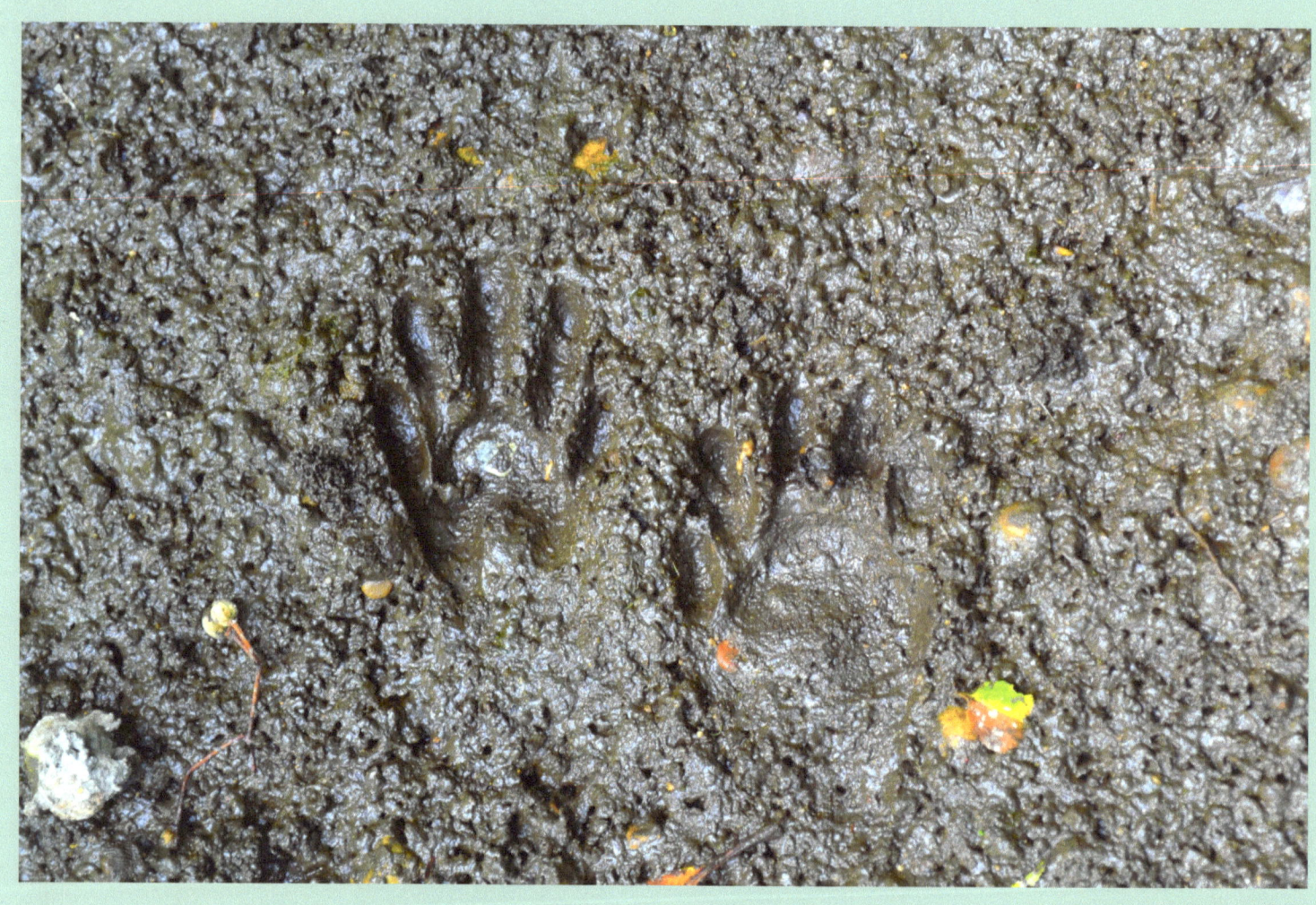

Photographer: Brittany Forgette

3.4 acres dedicated in 2008

Situated right along the Nippersink Creek and adjacent to land already protected by McHenry County Conservation District, this little parcel extends the amount of land set aside to remain wild and beautiful and adds a little more protection for our important water resources.

Spring Hollow Conservation Easement, Bull Valley

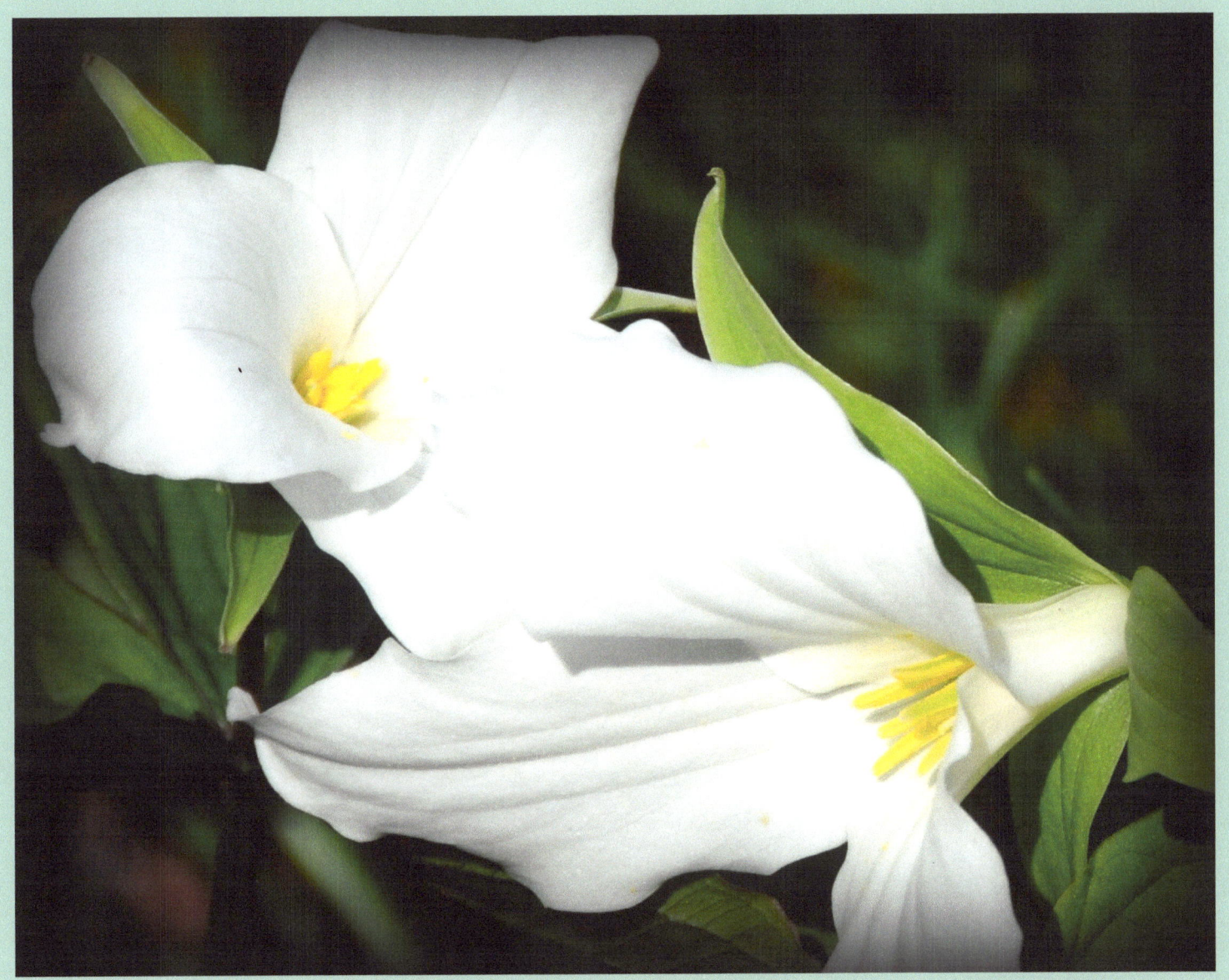

Photographer: Linda Gurgone

35 acres dedicated in 1977, transferred to TLC in 2013

Dick and Betty Babcock were the first Illinois family to dedicate a permanent conservation easement on their land in December 1977, making use of the law which Dick Babcock helped create. They named this place Spring Hollow for its many natural springs and rolling topography, and it is still in the family today.

Swanson Conservation Easement, Ringwood

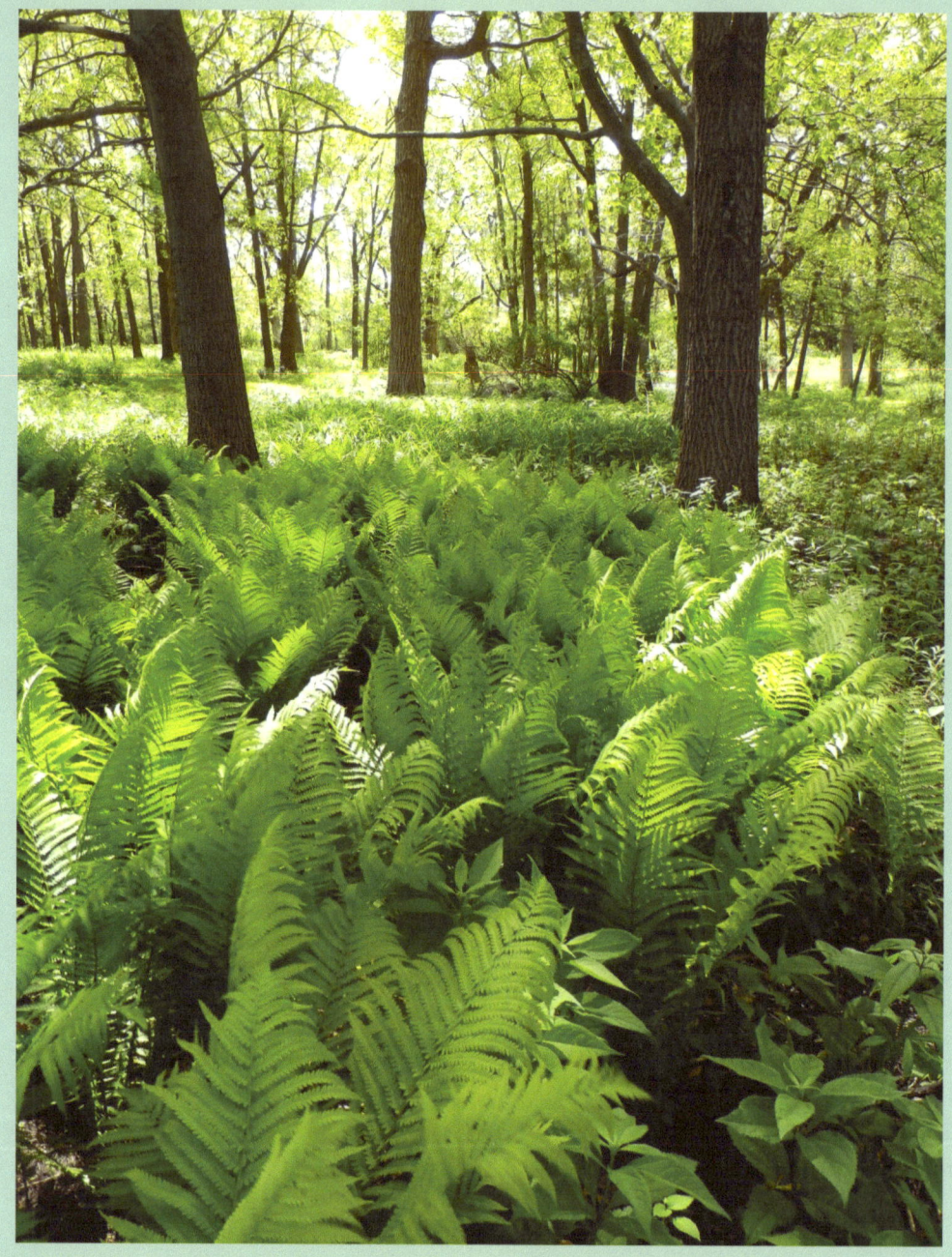

Photographer: Linda Santeler

4 acres dedicated in 2009

Walking paths wind through groves of oak trees and around ponds, all offering an astounding view of various spring wildflowers. Few backyards can boast the number of songbirds, frogs, and other critters that also call this their home. Thanks to years of careful tending and the foresight to dedicate an easement, this backyard will remain natural in perpetuity.

Van Maren Conservation Easement, Dunham Township

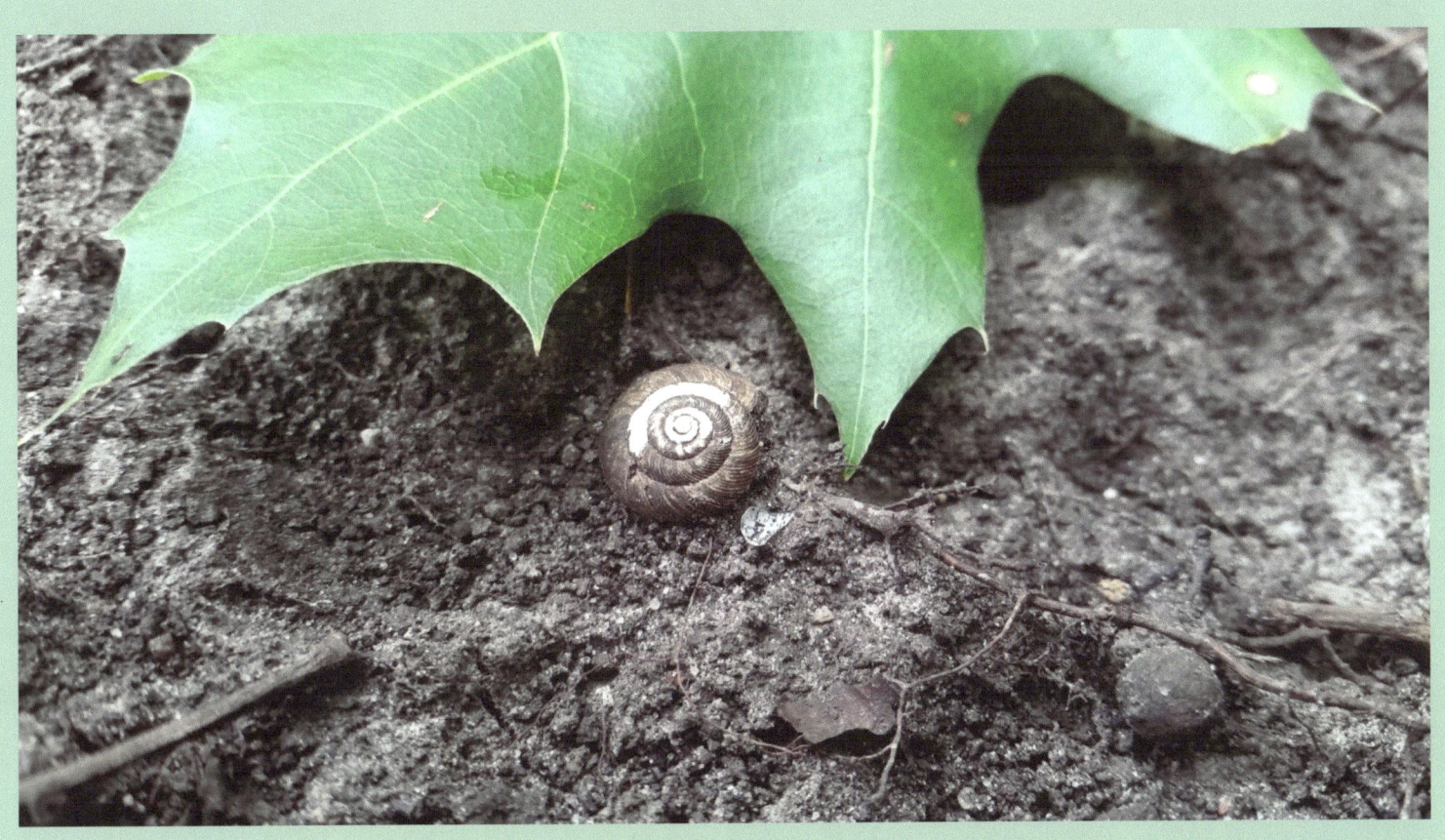

Photographer: Sarah Miller

40 acres dedicated in 2013

When Al Van Maren donated an easement on his 40 acres of woods, it helped preserve one of the last large remnant oak woodlands in the county. This woodland is part of a joint effort between McHenry County Conservation District and TLC to preserve a total of 93 contiguous acres of old growth oaks.

Waichunas Conservation Area, Nunda Township

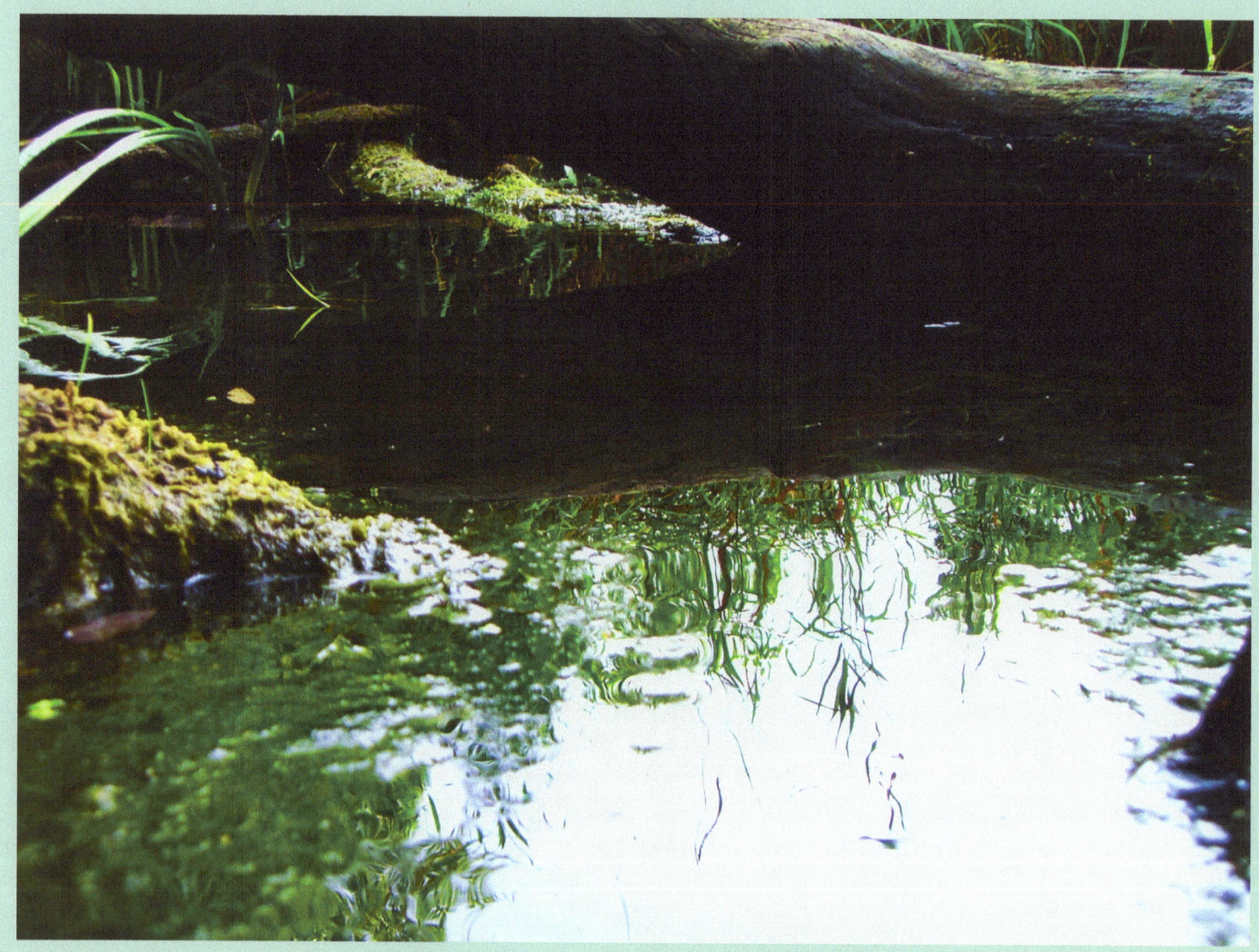

Photographer: Kathy Hammond

4 acres donated in 2002

During a 1997 survey, the Griswold Prairie area was identified as one of only a few remaining unprotected high quality natural areas in McHenry County. Peter Waichunas decided to donate this land to TLC, protecting an area for red-headed woodpeckers --a declining species.

Dorothy Weers Conservation Easement, Dorr Township

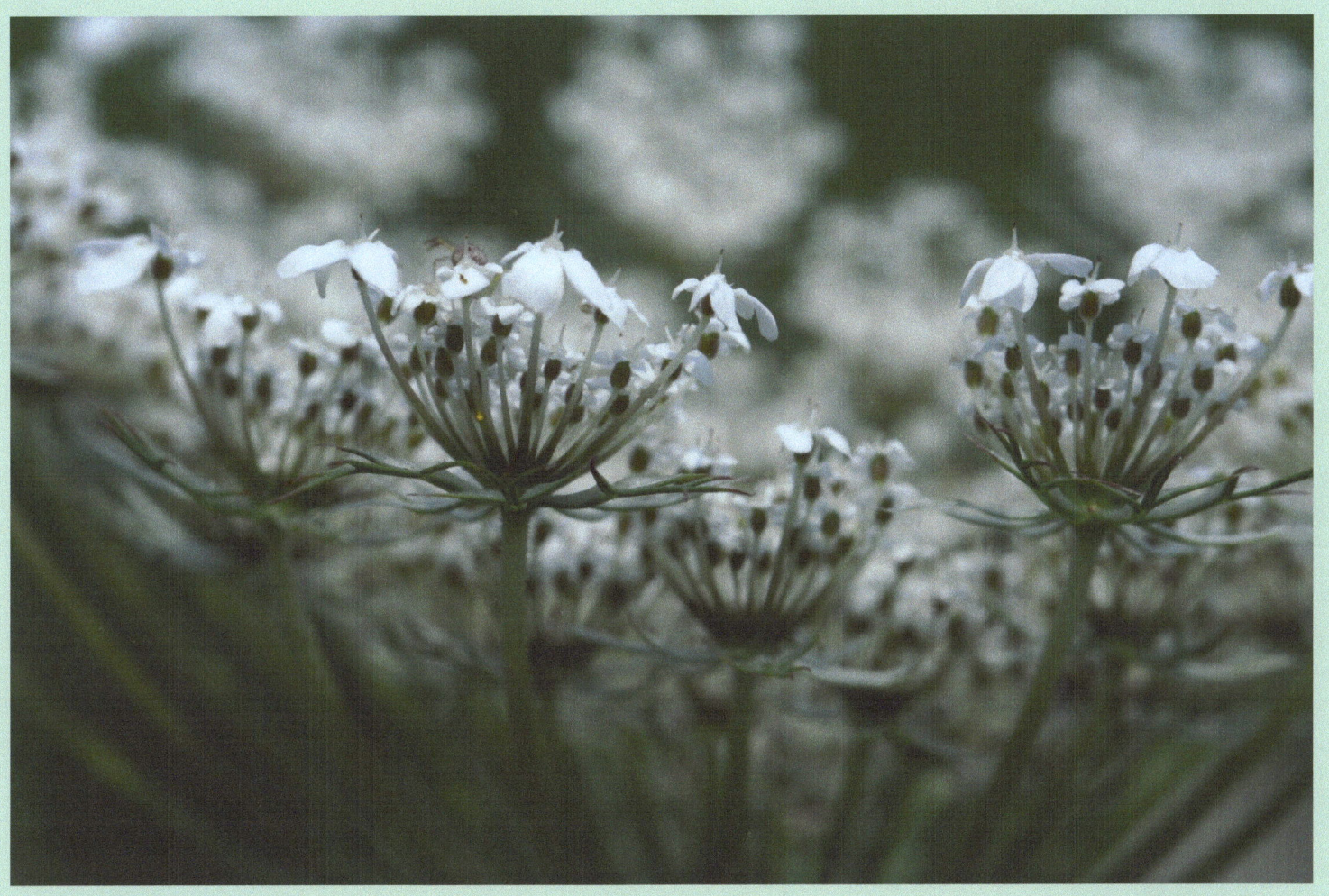

Photographer: Richard Ahrens

11 acres dedicated in 1993

Thirty-three acres of prairie, oak woodland and sedge meadow will remain undeveloped forever through the two conservation easements Dorothy Weers placed on the property she owned. While Dorothy is no longer with us, her legacy lives on as the new owners continue to care for the property

Westwood Conservation Area, Woodstock
Third Place

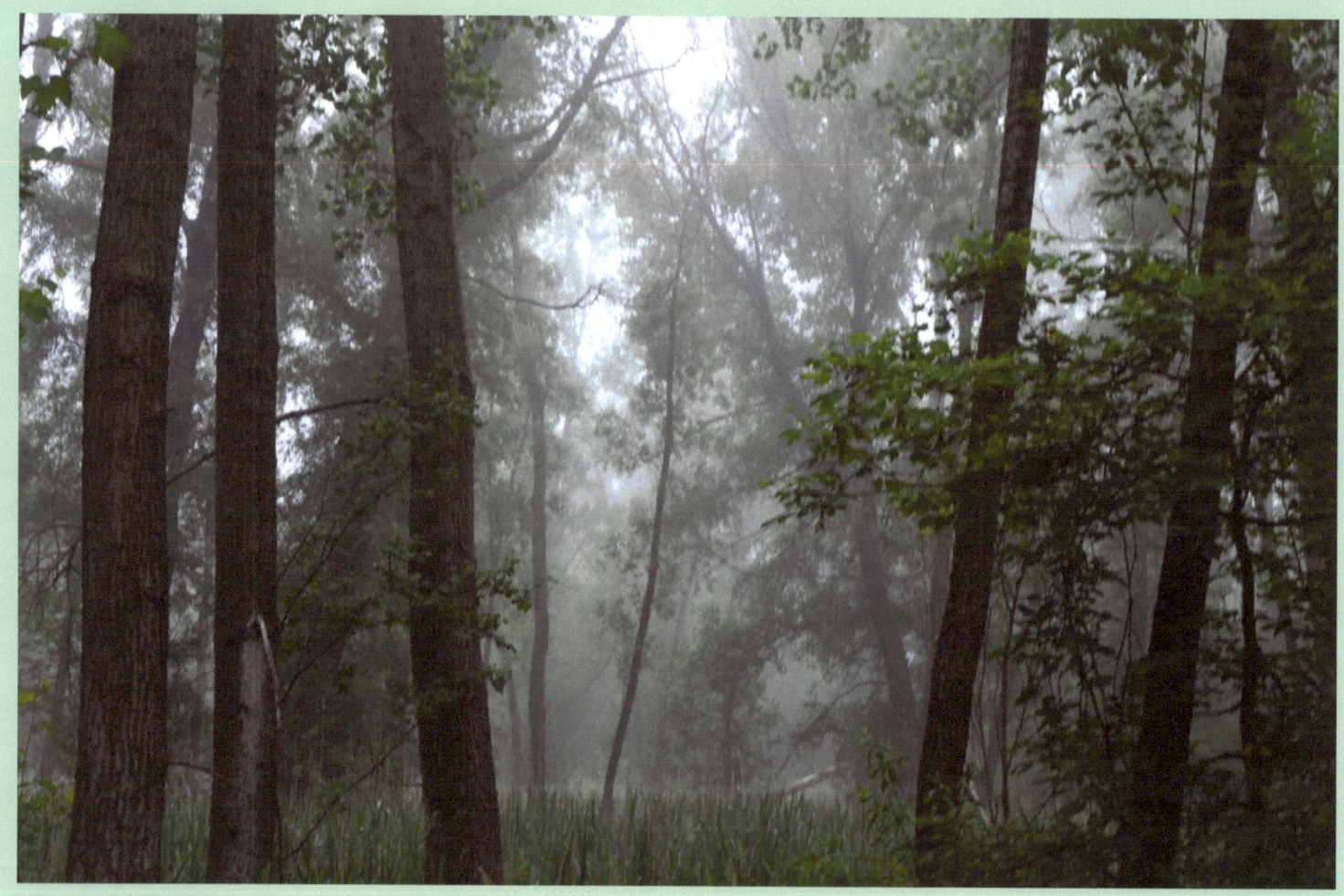

Photographer: Gail Moreland
63 acres owned by the City of Woodstock,
managed by TLC since 2006

In 2010 this property was dedicated as an Illinois Nature Preserve and buffer for the adjacent TLC Yonder Prairie. Restoration work has been underway for several years opening up the woodland full of massive oaks, and working along the edge to let it gently transition into prairie.

Wicker Conservation Easement, Alden Township

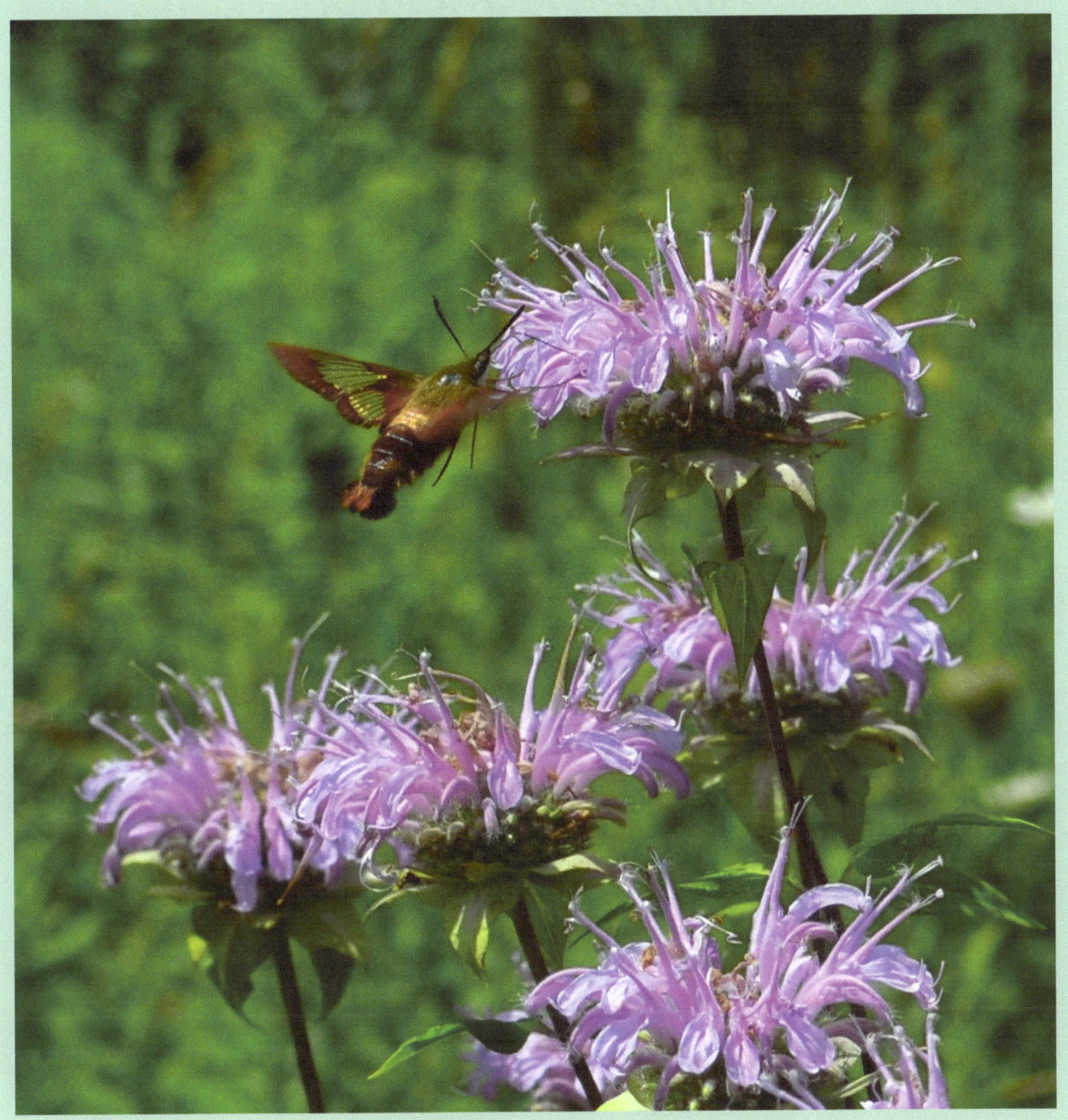

Photographer: Sue Boettcher
14 acres dedicated in 2003

When she purchased her farm, Nancy Wicker had the goal of fostering abused or neglected horses, but she also cared for the land. In 2001, she enrolled her property into the USDA's Wildlife Habitat Improvement Program, planted hundreds of native shrubs, and restored the wetlands.

Windy Knoll Conservation Area, Bull Valley
Honorable Mention

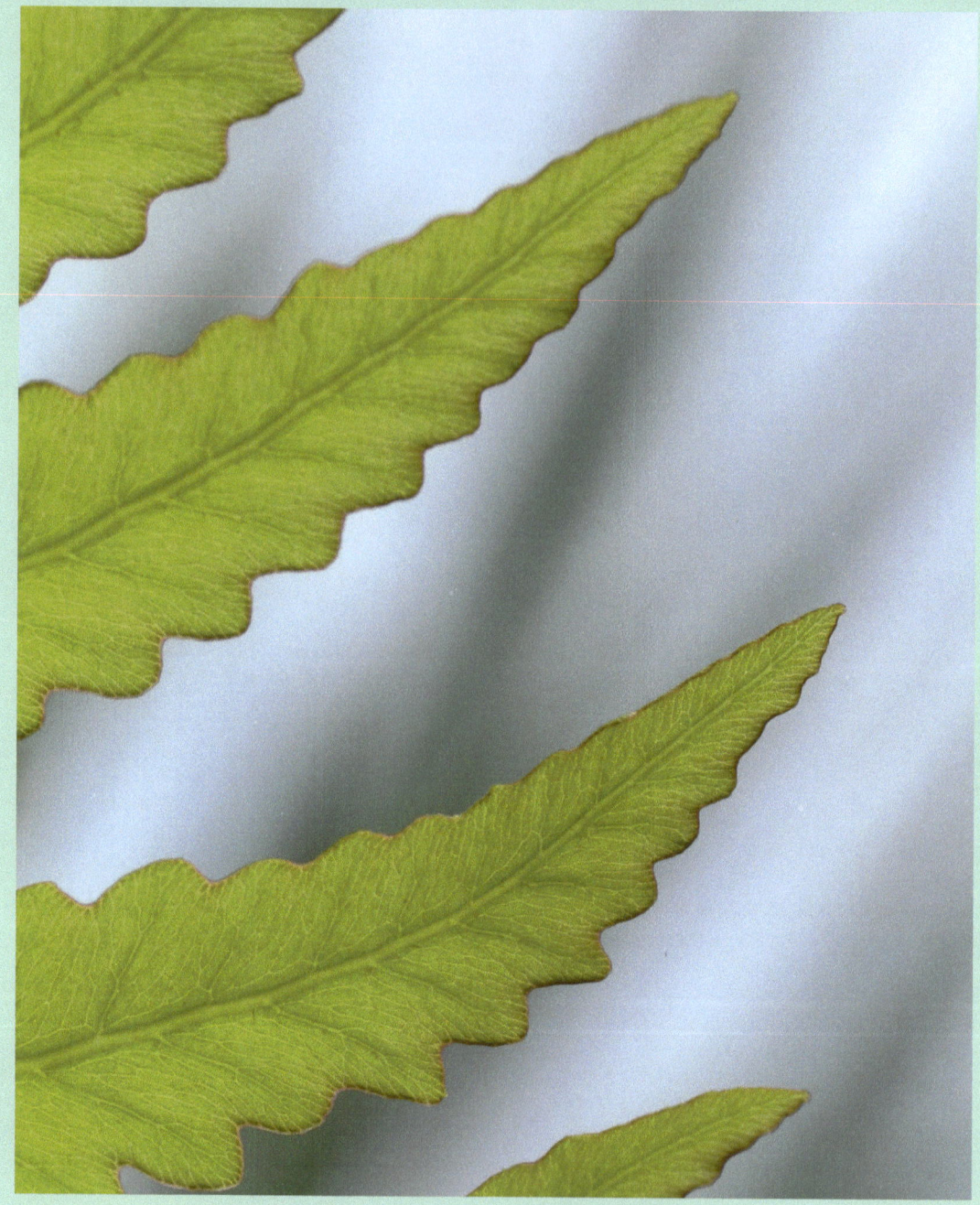

Photographer: Lisa McNerney
22 acres donated to TLC in 2002

Windy Knoll/Powers Creek was the first land donation that TLC accepted. This is another natural area right in the middle of a subdivision, allowing residents easy access to nature just outside their front doors.

Wingate Conservation Easement, Nunda Township

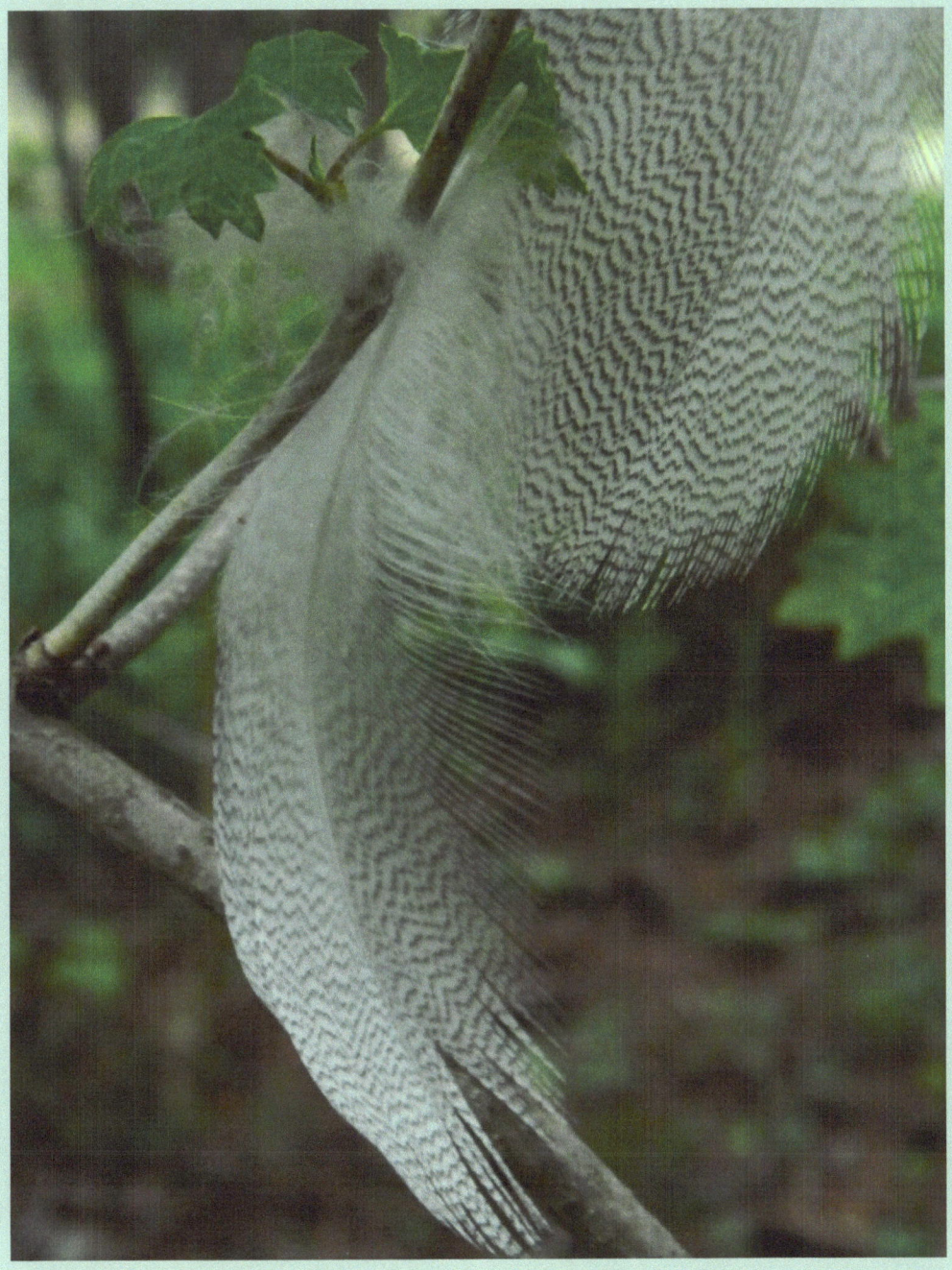

Photographer: Diana Floress

4 acres dedicated in 1994

Bill Wingate, famous for his "Wanders with Wingate" nature walks around McHenry County, lived on this property with his wife Ardath. They transformed their backyard into a wonderful place to enjoy their own nature walks, under the trees and along a stream.

Wonder Lake Sedge Meadow, Wonder Lake
People's Choice Winner, Friday

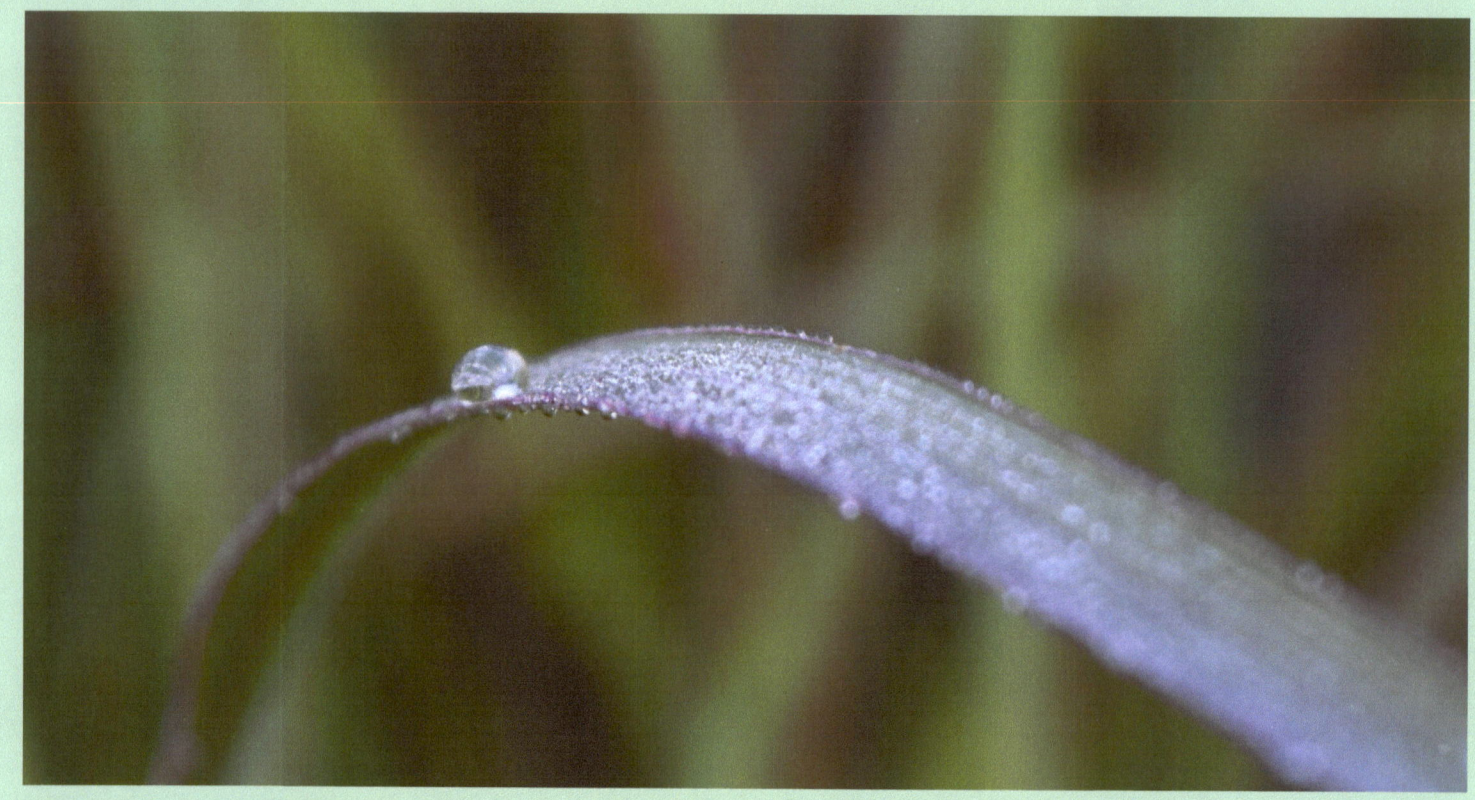

Photographer: Brianna Walneck
26 acres dedicated in 2006

This property provides a scenic overview of sedge meadow and oak savanna, with Wonder Lake itself in the background. Thanks to the easement, generations to come will be able to stand here and enjoy the same scenic vista.

Woodland Hills Conservation Easement, Lakewood

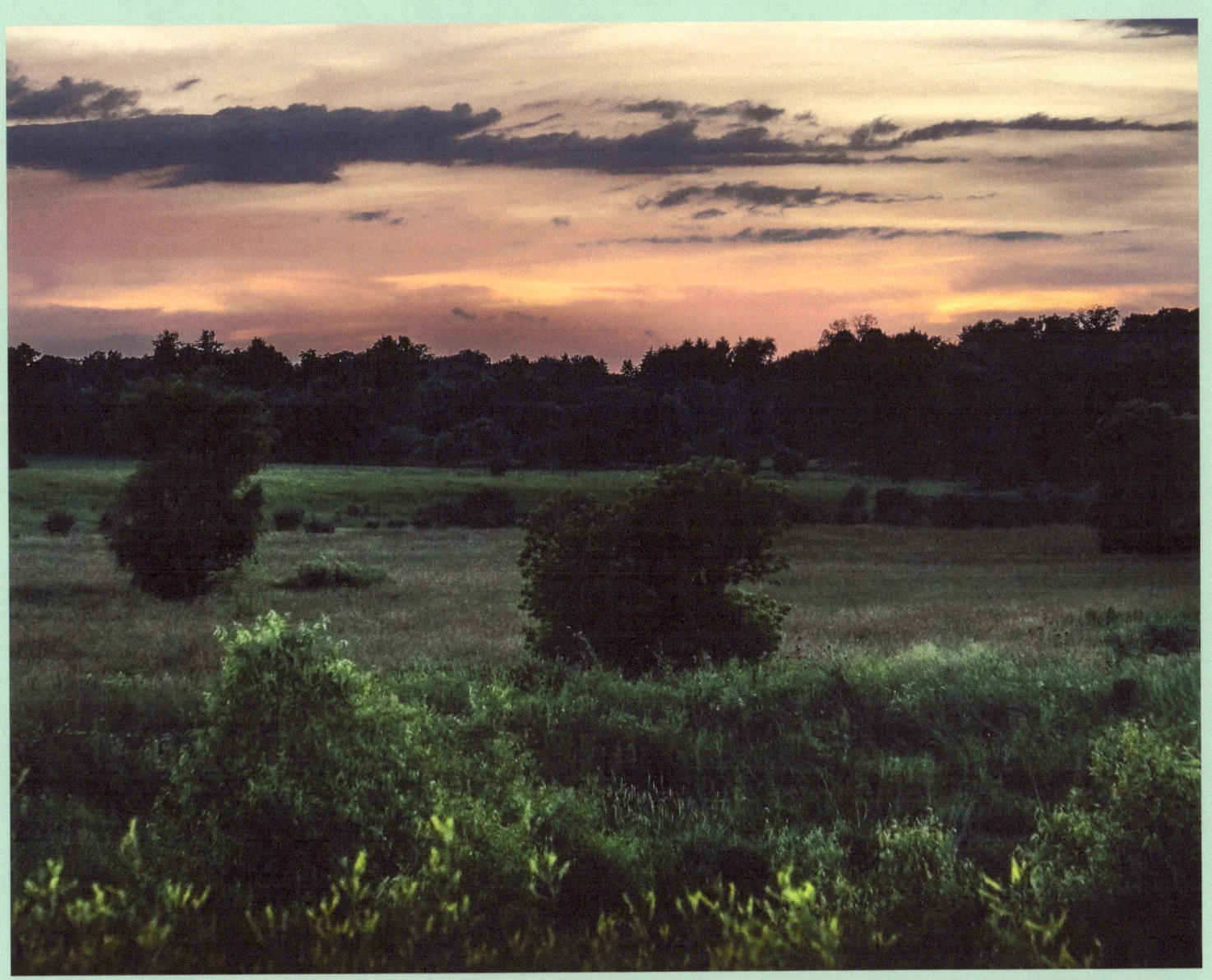

Photographer: Samantha Wyslak
58 acres dedicated in 2007

Near the corner of Ballard & Haligus Roads in Lakewood lies a 58 acre wetland and oak woods tucked in behind the Woodland Hills subdivision. While the surrounding development project has stalled with the economy, the wetland is as busy as ever providing critical habitat for birds, insects and local wildlife – and because of the conservation easement that the Village of Lakewood required, it will be available for nature forever!

Yonder Prairie Nature Preserve, Woodstock

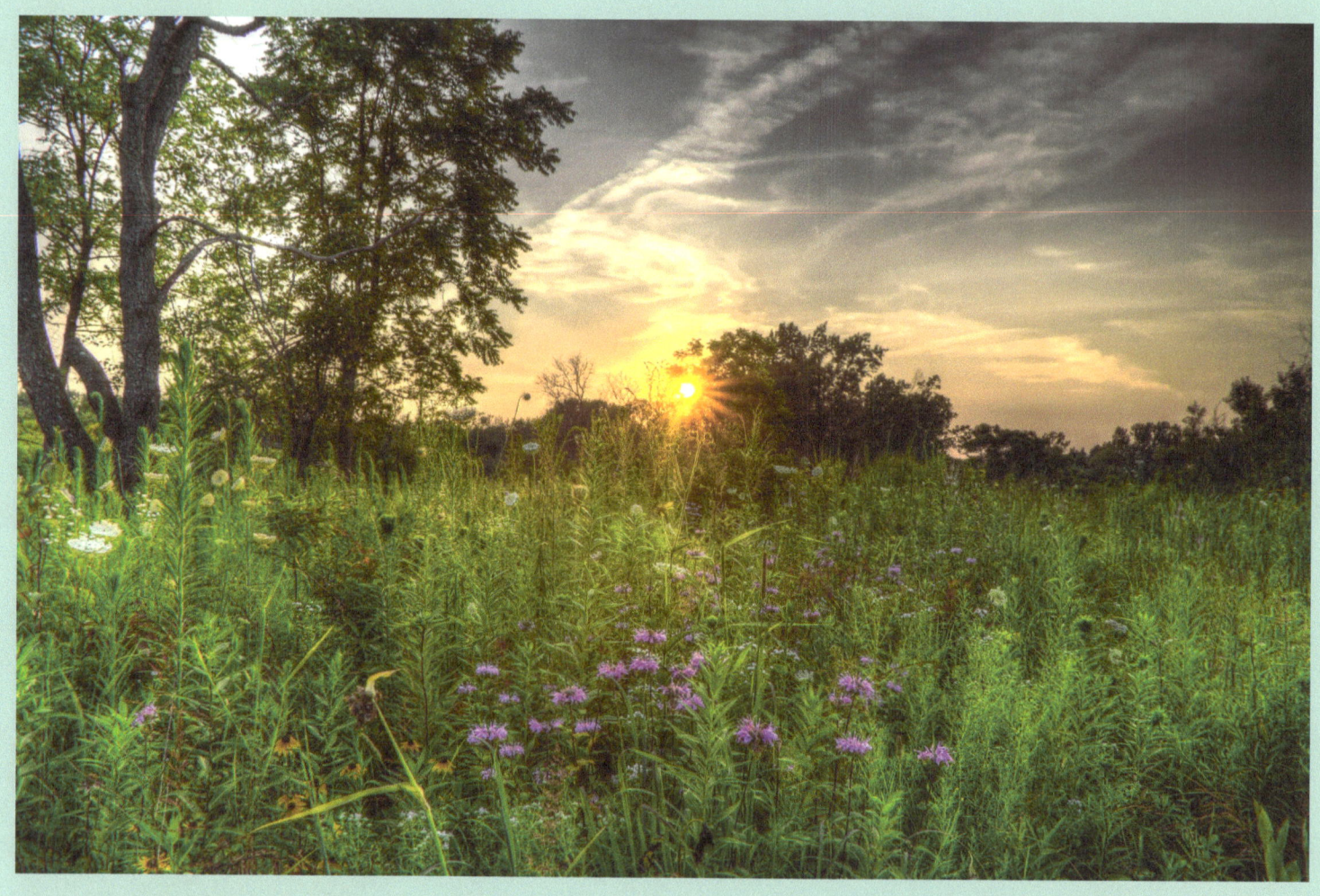

Photographer: Doug Frey

40 acres purchased by TLC in 2008

Prior to TLC's purchase of this land, it was deemed the highest quality unprotected natural area in the county. Now the complex of oak woodland, wet prairie and sedge meadow is classified as an Illinois Nature Preserve - the highest level of protection available to natural lands in the state.

Yonder Prairie Nature Preserve, Woodstock

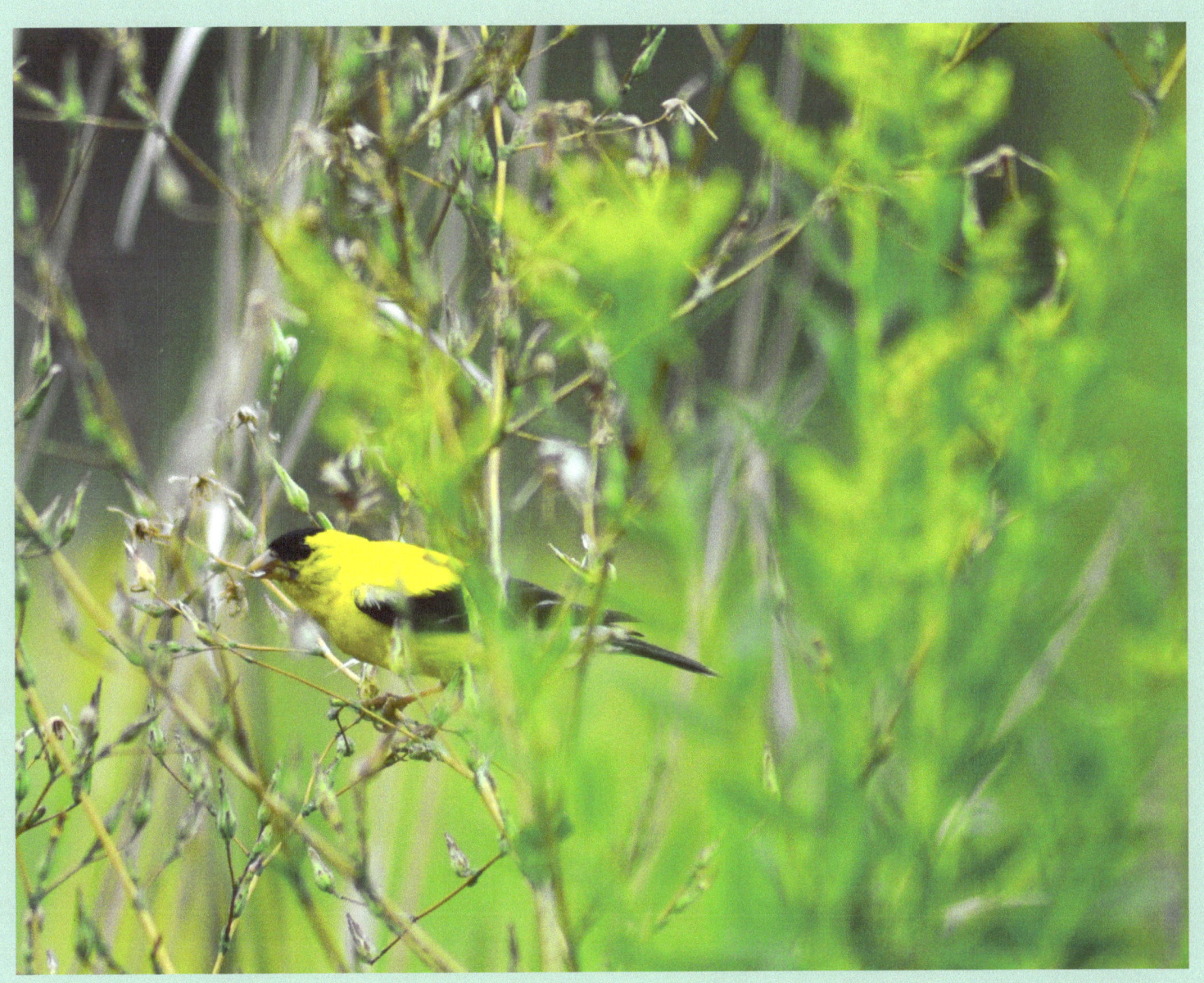

Photographer: Jennifer Luniewicz Martins

40 acres purchased by TLC in 2008

TLC is still working on increasing the amount of protected land surrounding Yonder Prairie. We helped protect about 100 acres on the south and east sides of the preserve, and just this summer added an additional 26 acres to Yonder Prairie to the west!

Zoost-Weier Conservation Area, Island Lake

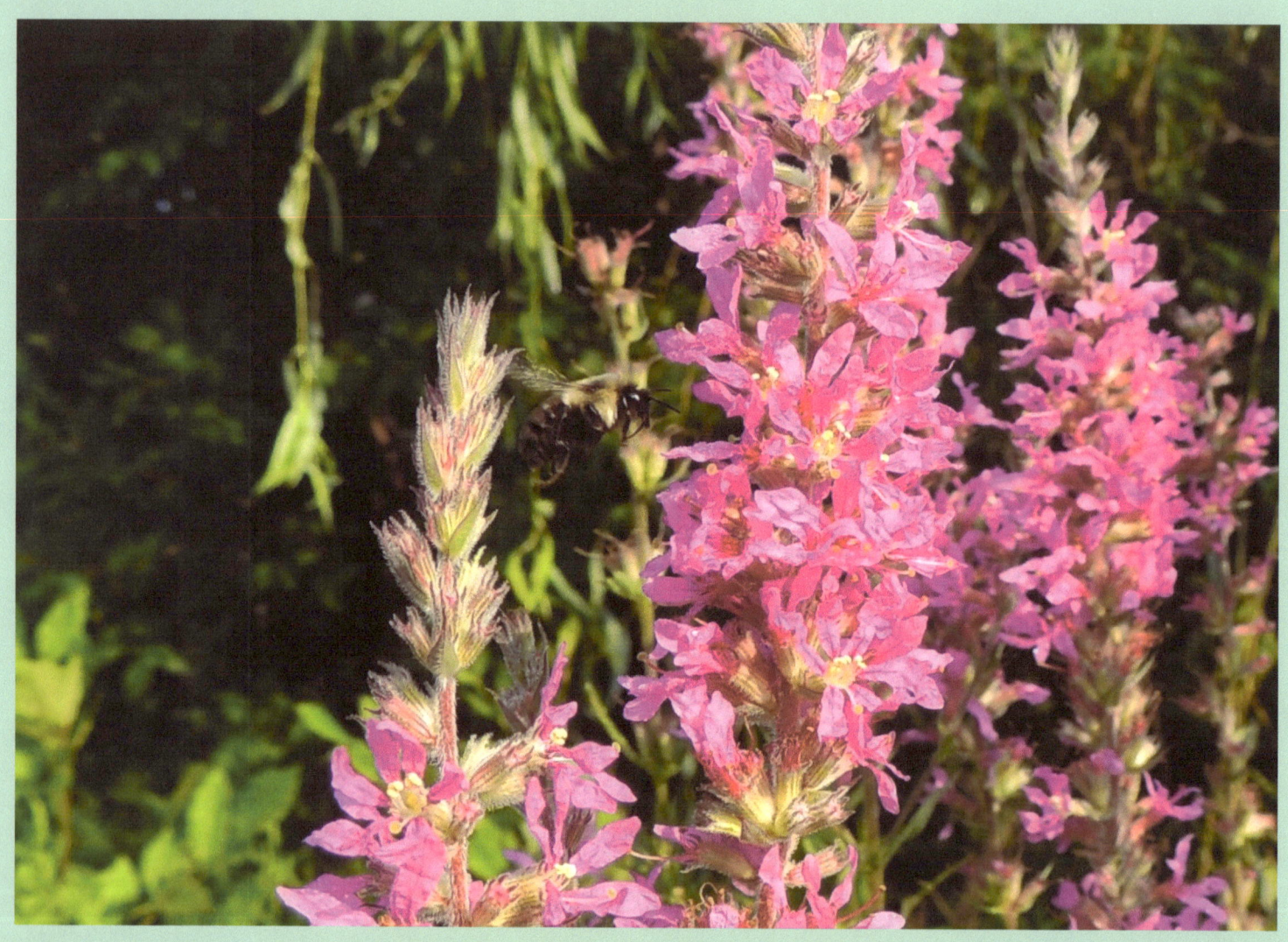

Photographer: Kendal Stephens

4 acres donated to TLC in 2011 & 2012

Carol and Matthew Zoost donated this parcel which includes hickory woods and a sedge meadow, providing wildlife habitat and visual appeal to people passing by on Roberts Road.

Zoost-Weier Conservation Area, Island Lake
Second Place

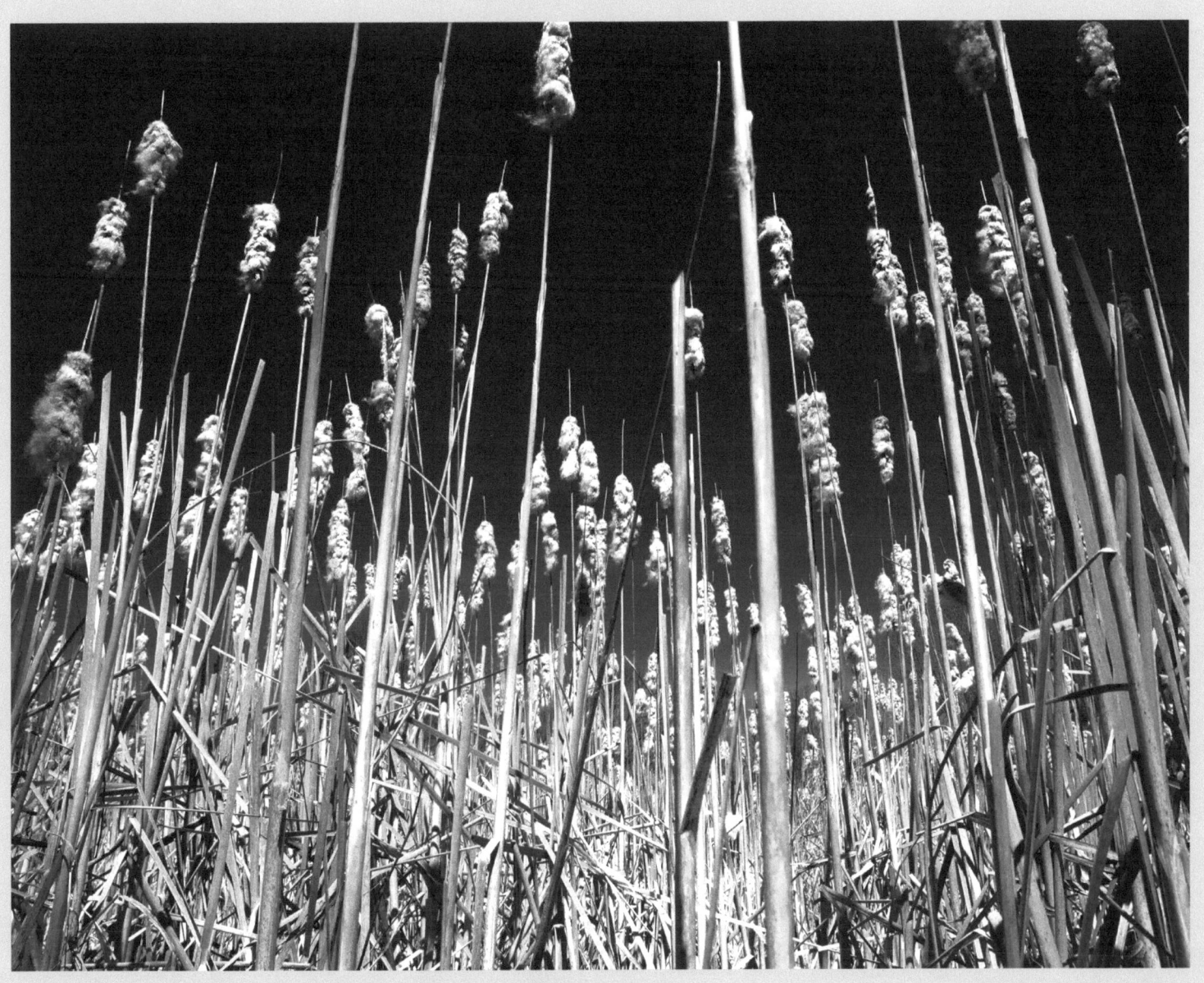

Photographer: Lisa Meinard-Sly

4 acres donated in 2011

Although we didn't quite know what we would find on this small corner of land, we were surprised with the vast amount of high quality remnant plants that still called this place home. With the help of our volunteers, TLC has gotten right to work restoring it.

Anderson Conservation Easement, Nunda Township
Landowner Winner

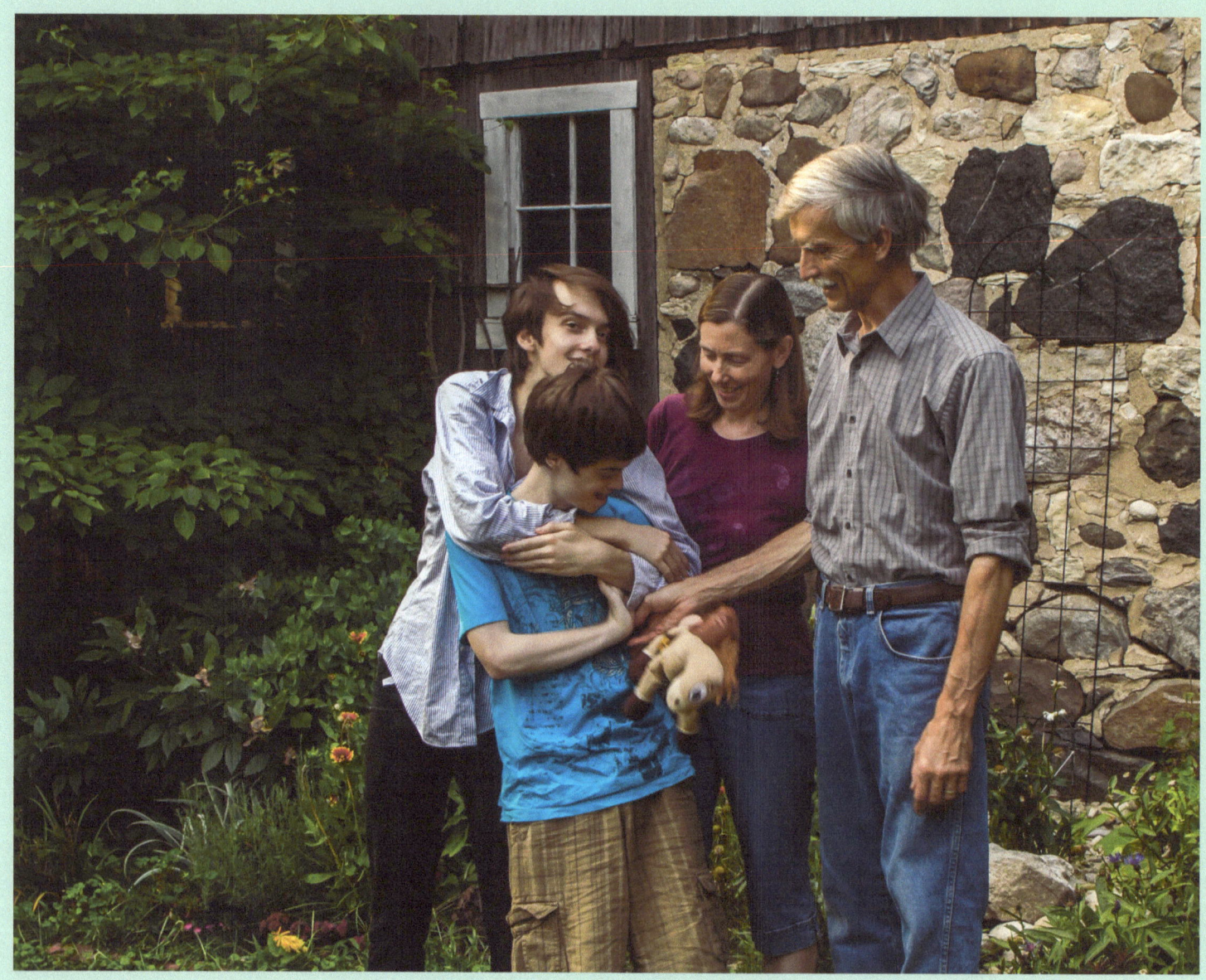

Photographer: Bob Williams
Landowners: Ders Anderson & Kathe Lacey-Anderson
2 acres dedicated in 1994

The Andersons were some of the first people in the county to place a voluntary easement on their land, helping to inspire preservation of the Powers Creek watershed. On the Anderson easement, paths lead all through their backyard, ducking around ponds, under trees, and through sweeping patches of native prairie plants.

TLC's Art of the Land Photo Contest

Each year since 2009, TLC invites amateur photographers to participate in a unique photo contest meant to highlight the inspiring nature of its land preservation work. The contest's goal is to introduce more local residents to the work of TLC and the beauty found in even small natural areas when one stops long enough to look.

TLC matches each photographer with a specific TLC property, providing them with the opportunity to visit the site throughout multiple seasons of the year. All photographs submitted are taken of properties on which TLC holds a conservation easement, land TLC owns or stewards, or of people who work with TLC for the purpose of preserving their land for the benefit of future generations.

For more information about Art of the Land, the Photo Contest, or The Land Conservancy, please visit www.ConserveMC.org.

TLC's 2014 Photo Contest was sponsored by Hey and Associates of Volo, Illinois. Thank you!

Hey and Associates, Inc.

Engineering, Ecology and Landscape Architecture

Volo Office: 26575 W. Commerce Drive, Suite 601, Volo, IL 60073
847.740.0888 | 847.740.2888 fax | volo@heyassoc.com

Chicago Office: 8755 W. Higgins Road, Suite 835, Chicago, IL 60631
773.693.9200 | 773.693.9202 fax | Chicago@heyassoc.com

Information about TLC's 2014
Art of the Land Art Sale and Benefit

2014 was the sixth year for TLC's Art of the Land Art Sale and Benefit at the Starline Building in Harvard. This two-night event, held in September, is a collaboration between artists from the region who find inspiration in the land and McHenry County's oldest non-profit land conservation organization: The Land Conservancy of McHenry County.

In 2014, the event started on Thursday with a live radio program called Voices of the Land, broadcast through Harvard Community Radio, www.harvardcommunityradio.com, hosted by storyteller Jim May, and featuring a conversation with landowners about their personal histories with the land.

Art of the Land could not happen without the many artists who donate 30% of their sales back to TLC to support its land preservation mission, and without the hundreds of guests who attend the event and purchase artwork.

Orrin and Karen Kinney, owners of the Starline Building, donate use of the space to TLC for the benefit, and donate the labor of several workers to help set up the space for this unique show.

It's worth noting that hundreds of volunteer hours (valued at several thousand dollars) are donated during the months leading up to the event. Volunteers do everything from hanging artwork, installing lighting, painting walls, serving food, selling tickets, sweeping floors, and coordinating live and silent auctions. Quite simply, Art of the Land could not happen without the efforts of all the volunteers.

Please contact TLC about participating at a future event:
815-337-9502 or www.ConserveMC.org.